MORE BOOKS FROM THE SAGER GROUP

The Stacks Reader Series

The Cheerleaders: A True Story, by E. Jean Carroll

An American Family: A True Story, by Daniel Voll

Flesh and Blood: A True Story, by Peter Richmond

An Accidental Martyr: A True Story, by Chip Brown

Death of a Playmate: A True Story, by Teresa Carpenter

The Detective: And Other True Stories, by Walt Harrington

Soldiers in the Army of God: A True Story, by Daniel Voll

Original Gangster: A True Story, by Paul Solotaroff

The Dreamer Deceiver: A True Story, by Ivan Solotaroff

Mary in the Lavender Pumps: A True Story, by Joyce Wadler

General Interest

The Stories We Tell:
Classic True Tales by America's Greatest Women Journalists

New Stories We Tell:
True Tales by America's New Generation of Great Women Journalists

Newswomen: Twenty-five Years of Front-Page Journalism

The Devil & John Holmes: And Other True Stories, by Mike Sager

Lifeboat No. 8: Surviving the Titanic, by Elizabeth Kaye

Hunting Marlon Brando: A True Story, by Mike Sager

Stopping the Road:
The Campaign Against a Trans-Sierra Highway, by Jack Fisher

The Living and the Dead, by Brian Mockenhaupt

More Books From The Sager Group

NOT GUILTY BY REASON OF AFGHANISTAN

AND OTHER TRUE STORIES

JOHN H. RICHARDSON

Not Guilty by Reason of Afghanistan: And Other True Stories

Published in the United States of America.

Cover design and cover art by WBYK.com.au
Interior design by Siori Kitajima, PatternBased.com

Cataloging-in-Publication data for this book
is available from the Library of Congress.

ISBN-13:
eBook: 978-1-950154-99-9
Paperback: 978-1-958861-00-4

Published by The Sager Group LLC
(TheSagerGroup.net)
In conjunction with NeoText
(NeoTextCorp.com)

The Stacks Reader Series #012

NOT GUILTY BY REASON OF AFGHANISTAN

AND OTHER TRUE STORIES

JOHN H. RICHARDSON

With an Introduction by Alex Belth

CONTENTS

JOHN H. RICHARDSON Q&A

By the time he was fourteen, John H. Richardson Jr. had already lived in four countries, including Vietnam, Greece, and the Philippines. That's when his father, who worked for the government, announced he had been reassigned to Korea. The boy could stay in the States and go to boarding school or join his parents in Korea, but the father decided his son was old enough to know the truth. Preposterous as it seemed, John H. Richardson Sr. was not a special assistant to the ambassador, as previously believed, but in fact worked for the C.I.A. Not just that, he'd been the Saigon bureau chief during the Vietnam War.

If a peripatetic childhood is not fertile enough ground for a career in journalism, a serious-minded but distant father with secrets—major secrets—will do the trick. Richardson has the detached, nonjudgmental, observational eye of the perpetual outsider. He's curious and smart, a realist with a spiky, mordant sense of humor; a truth-seeker, whether writing about abortion clinic doctors, gun advocates, or faded B-movie stars. Richardson loves characters on the fringe. "It's a privilege to listen to people tell their stories and write them down," he says, "especially when they're the kind of people who get overlooked."

First at Premiere magazine and then for Esquire—with plenty of freelance stops in between—Richardson amassed a trove of memorable pieces, as a terrific reporter and a first-class storyteller. Don't let the remove fool you; there is plenty of heart and morality in Richardson's tougher pieces. For the most part, though, his morality revolves around the challenges of his craft—"in just looking closely and trying to get things right."—Alex Belth

Q: You had an international upbringing, correct? How did your childhood help prepare you for being a journalist?

JHR: I was born in Washington, D.C., moved to Greece when I was eight months old, to the Philippines when I turned four, to Vietnam at eight, then a four-year stint back in D.C. before moving to Korea. With every move, I confronted a new culture, each with different traditions and mores. In the Department of Defense international schools, one of the first things they taught was that we should try to understand our new world before we made any judgments. In Korea, the lesson focused on "three men on a shovel," a Korean way of digging trenches that our soldiers ridiculed until the Koreans proved that three men with one shovel (two using ropes tied to the shovel) can move more dirt than three men with three shovels. You become obsessed with mapping the territory—do I bring the soup bowl to my lips or leave it on the table? Great training for a journalist.

Q: What was it like being a teenager on an army base?

JHR: I was an embassy brat, not an army brat. We had a cook, two maids, and a full-time chauffer who took my dad to work in a black limousine. Plus, I had a black passport, which gave me diplomatic immunity and drove the Korean soldiers who manned the checkpoints after curfew insane. Big difference.

Q. Did you always feel like an American over there?

JHR: Conspicuously so. I mean, people would come up to me in the street and ask if they could touch my hair.

Q. So what about when you went back to the States? Did you feel like an outsider?

JHR: A friend of mine from Korea said something when she left about how weird it was to be going to the place "where I'm supposed to belong." The first time I came back to stay, I was ten, and I had to learn to cuss as protective coloration—a few fucks and shits, and I was one of the boys, egging cars, shoplifting, drinking: oh, to belong and not to belong. Because, yeah, I always felt like an outsider. "Third culture kids," they call us. The flip side is seeing, over and over, humanity's best trait, the kindness people show to strangers, which almost makes that lonely, detail-hungry outsider feeling worth it, almost.

Q: And the downside?

JHR: Well, I guess I like to think of myself as freer in my mind than more embedded people, less captured by cultural biases and assumptions. I annoy girlfriends by calling myself a "lone mobile unit," a phrase I picked up from Brian Eno. There's some pride in that, some arrogance too, and probably some confusions of identity. And loneliness. And a troubling sense of detachment. In other words, it's exactly like being a writer.

Q: When did you first become aware of what we now call long-form magazine journalism? Did you read *Rolling Stone* as a kid?

JHR: In Korea, the U.S. Army library had copies of The Village Voice Reader and, astonishingly, Evergreen, a wild beatnik-cum-hippie magazine that I think might have been created by Barney Rosset, publisher of Beckett and Genet. They didn't make me want to be a journalist though, maybe because the prose wasn't that inspiring. I studied literature in grad school, wrote and published short stories. Then I decided to drop out of grad school and my mother-in-law suggested I try journalism, hooking me up with the editor of Corrections magazine, who sent me to a fancy hunting lodge to listen to rich old white guys talk about prison reform. I loved it. Going out, meeting people, asking questions, soaking up the little details, going back to my desk to think about it and write it up. But I still thought of it mostly as a job, until I started rereading people like Joan Didion and Michael Herr, whom I admired when I read as an undergrad but didn't connect to anything I might want to do. They showed me what was possible, and I never looked back.

Q: What was your first job in journalism?

JHR: Actually, that was in Korea. I was fifteen, and the U.S. Army gave me a summer job as a photographer. I learned that having a camera in your hands makes you look at things much more carefully, which was weirdly exciting. Capturing the fleeting moment had and still has a primal appeal for me. And my shots of the Israeli ambassador performing the lead role in Harold Pinter's The Caretaker were on display in the theater lobby opening night, which was pretty cool. But not as cool as working as a police reporter for the Albuquerque Tribune, which is still probably the most fun job I ever had. I would show up at the police department at five a.m., pick the night's most colorful crimes out of the police blotter and go out to flesh them out—oh man, the guy who got arrested stealing toys to give his kids for Christmas! The woman who tried to rob a bank to pay her boyfriend's debts by holding a bottle of nail polish in her pocket so it looked like a gun! The one-legged hooker who specialized in older guys! "It says in the Bible that you can't offend the Lord in the flesh," she told me. The man-caught-in-a-stairwell-fucking-a-grapefruit story, I still mourn that one. My editors were like, "Are you kidding? No way we're publishing that." I went back to the PD to commiserate with the cop who made the arrest, and he had the cored-out grapefruit on his desk in a plastic bag. He asked if I wanted it, so I took it to the newsroom and put it on the news editor's desk.

Q: Before that, did you go to college?

JHR: Oh man, that's a long story. Basically, I dropped out of high school after tenth grade, moved to Hawaii, bought a motorcycle, wrecked the motorcycle, applied to college, got into college, dropped out of college, got busted, did a couple of weeks in a charming "youth correctional facility" where one of the guards had a hook for a hand, went back to Korea—diligently working on the flap copy for my future books, in other words. I was planning on spending the next few years wandering around Asia when I got a letter from my sister saying I'd been accepted by USC, which came as a complete surprise to me since I hadn't applied. She got my test scores and filled out the forms without telling me. Apparently she thought I'd end up in a Thai prison, which probably wasn't a bad guess. So much for my book about life in a Thai prison!

Q: What did you make of L.A. when you first got there?

JHR: I don't remember any first impressions about L.A., but I have a vivid memory of getting off the plane and seeing my sister and her roommate waiting for me, because that roommate was a shimmering vision of beauty in a sexy summer dress. Wearing makeup. They took me to a party put on by students at the famous USC drama department and most of them were wearing makeup too, boys included. They seemed kind of white-bread to me, more Neil Simon than Samuel Beckett, but, you know, they wore makeup. They were lively, even antic. I ended up with a double major in English and theater and, years later, almost married the roommate. And learned to love L.A. in all its tawdry glory.

Q: How long were you in New Mexico working for a newspaper?

JHR: I worked in Albuquerque for two years, then a friend turned down a job covering the film industry for the L.A. Daily News and suggested me. I was making about $22,000, and the Daily News was offering $35,000, the film industry seemed like a fun thing to cover, so I jumped at it. Unfortunately, the people who ran the Daily News were dicks, including my editor— a woman but a huge dick. My first week she tried to get me to put my byline on a wire story. "Just change some of the words," she said. I refused, and another reporter told the editor in chief, who overruled her. Things went downhill from there.

Q: How did you make the transition to *Premiere*?

JHR: Kim Masters recommended me. She was the reporter who went to the EIC about the wire story, and she'd just gotten a job there. So I started pitching freelance pieces. The first one they accepted was about a Foley artist, which is a person that adds ambient sounds to a soundtrack, a fact I learned the night before I pitched it. Looking back at it now, the opening sentence cracks me up. " 'These are my slut shoes,' says Alicia Stevenson, holding up a truly hideous pair of wedge-heeled sandals, all cracked and covered with duct tape." That's me. Then I did a piece about Angelyne, the mysterious woman who had plastered her "trash sex-goddess image, complete with teased blond hair and torpedo bust" all over Hollywood at the cost of $8.3 million dollars even though she didn't act or sing. "I really don't want to be famous for being an actress," she told me. "I want to be famous for the magic I possess." I guess it was seeing all those bar girls in Korea at fourteen, I've always loved louche underworld characters and oddballs in general. I hated doing movie stars. A friend's wife once said, "I get it, you like to write about subcultures." She was right, except they're all subcultures to me. Anyway, a job opened up a year later, and I called the boss and lied that I was coming to N.Y.C. for some other thing, would she have time to see me? Spent my last $600 on a plane ticket and a Macy's sports coat. Didn't get the job. But two months later, the guy who did got fired and the boss—the great and wonderful Susan Lyne—called me. That was the turning point for me. If Susan hadn't been the kind of editor she was, I might have traded journalism for a real job. But she let me off the leash, and I ran with it.

Q: How did you like covering Hollywood?

JHR: Looking back, it was a blast. There were so many colorful people, and nobody else seemed all that interested unless they were famous. My early features were about a ruthless young screenwriter pushing a sentimental script and a wild-man producer who'd pissed off almost everybody in Hollywood. The one I consider my breakthrough piece was about a young guy who quit a very good job at Warner Brothers to produce a low-budget action movie and sell it to the international rug merchants in the underworld of the Cannes Film Festival. Susan actually sent me all the way to Cannes to follow him around for a week, one of the most exhausting and exhilarating experiences of my life so far, and I wanted to capture the intensity of the experience in prose somehow. But I couldn't do it. I had a windowless office that was basically just a desk and wallboard, basically a large closet, and I sat there for days and days, producing nothing and slowly going insane. Frustration always plays a large part in my getting-started process. One day after lunch I was skimming through a short-lived magazine called Future Sex, reading a piece on a prototype for something called "tele-dildonics," and I had this sudden impulse to just say "Fuck it" and kick out the jams. I turned to the keyboard of my giant early-1990s computer and blasted off the first five hundred words faster than I could type:

I think there's a little skin between the blisters on my feet, but I can't find it because I don't have a microscope. I've been in Cannes two days, and I feel as if I'm a month into the Bataan Death March. I got three hours' sleep last night, and that's three hours more than my friend Alan Schechter, who hasn't slept for thirty-six hours. After we close down the discos, he's been sneaking off to the bed of a Norwegian girl. He thinks I don't know, but investigative reporting is my life. And here he is now, all of twenty-six years old and scrawny as a Mexican pariah dog, leading a meeting with two European millionaires and two of Hollywood's top lawyers. "Savage has closed," he says, "payment accepted. As regards to the other screenplay—the producer who gave it to us still doesn't know we slipped it to the studios. His last comment to me was 'Alan, I know we're all friends.' " ...

I'm not saying that's genius, or even modern—the echoes of Kerouac and Wolfe are obvious—but the experience of blasting the words out and having them "come out almost in their form," as some other writer once said of those blessed moments—freed me up. Susan must have seen it too because right after she read that piece, she called me up and said, "Would you be interested in writing a serialized novel in Premiere?"

Q: How did you go from *Premiere* to *Esquire* during its great run in the late '90s and through the 'aughts under editor in chief David Granger?

JHR: Granger called me up one day, said he'd heard I was a good writer, and asked me to go to lunch. This was when he was number two at GQ. He ended up asking me to do a story about my father, which took me six months and ran over fifteen thousand words. He killed it. A year or so later, Susan told me I could do better for myself as a freelancer and offered to hook me up with Kurt Andersen, who was running New York magazine at the time. Maybe I could split my time between the two magazines? I trusted her completely and wanted to write about other stuff than just Hollywood. So I quit the steady paycheck and pension, and Kurt sent me to Peru to do Lori Berenson, the college girl from New York City who joined a Latin American revolutionary group called the Tupac Amaru, and put the story on the cover. Then he got fired. Around the same time, Susan left Premiere for ABC, and her replacement fired me. Suddenly I had two little kids and half the salary, wonderful. Then someone told me about Granger taking over at Esquire, so I went over to the old Esquire offices and told him he had to hire me. He gave me that dubious and pained expression he uses, the "I suffer because I work with writers" expression and gave me a contract. So I worked at both places for a couple of months or two, then I quit New York to give Esquire my full attention. A couple of pieces later, Granger made me a "writer at large," the perfect job description as far as I'm concerned.

Q: Again, you've written about celebrities such as George Clooney and Angelina Jolie, reported from the set of James Cameron's *Titanic*, but many of your most gripping stories tell the stories of people we've never heard of. Is there anything in particular that draws you to true crime pieces?

JHR: When it comes to crime stories, my year as a police reporter in New Mexico had a huge influence. The charms of petty crime I've already talked about (although there's certainly a long literary tradition of that too). But I got to know a cop who shot a fleeing suspect who turned out to be a harmless twenty-one-year-old kid. The kid's death still haunted him, but he also showed me pictures of what the inmates did to each other during the New Mexico Prison Riot, like driving a metal bar through a man's ear and out of his mouth. What a complex message that was—grief, defiance, anger, and a plea for understanding. People reveal themselves under pressure, that's always been a crime-story cliché. Another influential moment was when my editors asked me to do something about gangs. I drove up to a bunch of—can I say "cholos"?—standing under a bridge in their wifebeaters and bandanna headbands and asked if they'd talk to me. Blank stares, uncomfortable silence, finally one spoke up. "Can you get us jobs?"

So I realized there's "cheese down that hole," as an old friend used to say. Like sex, it can take you deep. And each story is its own universe. Wasp Woman caught my eye because the details were so baroque—the star of a Roger Corman movie about an aging beauty who takes wasp hormones to stay young giving birth in real life to a dwarf son and enrolling him in an experimental program at UCLA where he was given growth hormones? Are you kidding me? The kid was being sentenced for her murder at the San Fernando Valley Courthouse. I'd never been there. It turned out to be a classic example of art-deco sandstone from the 1930s, probably built by the WPA. The hearing room was big, with dark wooden benches. Her psychiatrist told the court he often felt like killing her, too, a prison official said the poor boy was cooperative in every way, the judge said his mom brought it on herself and let him go. From there it just kept getting more and more twisted. And sad.

"Death of a Small-Timer" started about a year before it became a story. On the suggestion of a B-movie actress I knew, I went to the little talent office on Santa Monica where this natty old man sat behind his old wooden desk, his parrot standing at his elbow like a sentry. He showed me his model books and talked about the time Demi Moore walked in off the street, stripping down for some sample shots right there in the back with the prison cell and clawfoot bathtub movie sets, just like all his other clients. Nothing for me there. But a year later my friend called me up and said the cops found him dead with his safe open and some of his cheesecake models were teaming up to find out who killed him. I couldn't resist that. But Granger killed it, which frustrated me so much I wrote it about five more times trying to get it right.

"The Grifters" started with a piece in Variety about the very sketchy collapse of a movie starring a sketchy unknown named Sonny Gibson. I tracked the director down and he told me Sonny told him not to backlight him because he had a twenty-one-inch dick. He also gave me a lead to the widow he conned out of a million bucks while her husband lay dying in a hospital. Then I found the farmer in Kansas who let him burn down a cornfield for another of his Springtime for Hitler-type scams. That story was pure lurid fascination, although with a touch of moral outrage here and there as I met the victims.

Q: Do you often feel led by a moral imperative in reporting and telling these stories?

JHR: Led by a moral imperative? God no. I'm not proud of that, it's just my nature. It's always about the story. Sometimes I'm reluctant because of a moral sense, like not wanting to have put myself in the presence of someone like Newt Gingrich or Charlton Heston. But doing the stories could change that, especially when Granger and Warren [Mark Warren, then Esquire's executive editor] started assigning me stories on topics like race and abortion. I wanted to do the best I could for Mike Brown Sr., who was so decent and suffered so much. The suffering patients at the Boulder Abortion Clinic and Jackson Women's Health are something I'll never forget. I got caught up by climate change. But my response to that was mostly just trying to make the prose worthy of them. Bill McKibben I'm not, obviously, but I do think there's a kind of morality in just looking closely and trying to get things right. It's a privilege to listen to people tell their stories and write them down, especially when they're the kind of people who get overlooked. That's why I tend to say yes to anything, because I believe there's a story in everyone. And you should be open to surprise—when I was starting at Esquire, Granger asked me if I wanted to do "the little people." I said, "Hell yes," thinking he wanted me to do gas station attendants and store clerks. He sent me to a dwarf convention. Not exactly people who get overlooked, actually the opposite, but I got a book out of it. And Chuck Heston turned out to be a lovely guy, very much an actor, courtly with strangers. His dad was a small-town sheriff, ergo the gun love, but at dinner he told me showbiz stories like a charming old queen.

DEATH OF A SMALL-TIMER

Hal was an old-time Hollywood agent, forever at the desk of his little storefront movie studio on Santa Monica in his neat white shirt and dyed hair and that famous parrot by his side. He would do bondage but drew the line at porn. "I have a philosophy about that," he said. "I'll degrade women up to a point, and no more." When the cops found his body next to his open safe, everyone had the same question: "What happened to the bird?"

The first time I talk to her, on the phone from another city, she tells me that she loved Hal, she'd be happy to talk about him. Like everyone, she is troubled by his mysterious death. She met him when the big parts dried up and hardcore came in, and he sent her out for ten years, he sent her out and got her lots of work. Hal was always a gentleman and never looked her up and down, always so gracious. "He'd say, 'I got you the audition, you got the part yourself.' " He sent her out on a lot of girlie stuff and bit movie parts and later private photo sessions with fans of her old cult movies. And he was a sweet old man, always sitting there at the desk of his little storefront movie studio on that bleak stretch of Santa Monica Boulevard, a real old-time Hollywood character in a neat white shirt and dyed hair and his famous parrot, a macaw, sitting on the edge of his desk. A lot of times she'd shoot right there, on the sets he had rigged up in the back, boudoir and prison cell, rock 'n' roll band, clawfoot bathtub, doctor's office. But work tapered off in the 1990s and she hadn't seen him for a few years.

The next time I call, she seems confused. When I drive through the blank glare of Los Angeles daylight to the flatlands below Hollywood and find her little stucco building, she opens the door wearing an old blue bathrobe. The famous boobs are gone. She has dull hammered eyes, like someone still drunk from the night before. She takes my hands and kisses my fingers like I'm a priest come to pay a death visit. She leads me into a little two-bedroom apartment that stinks of cat pee. When we sit she looks confused for a minute, then slips her hand into my lap. "Uh, that's okay," I say, something like that.

She seems puzzled. "I don't even know why you're here," she says.

I tell her I'm here for Hal, to ask questions about Hal Guthu. I met him once, liked him, wanted to look into his death. She digs through her Filofax for people I can call.

Then she stops, puzzled again. "Why are you here?"

For Hal, I say. And she starts talking about his pictures, the old stills he had of Marilyn Monroe that no one had ever seen. His collection of early cheesecake movies. She seems to believe that someone killed him to steal this stuff. "They're all gone," she says sadly.

"But why would someone kill him for old movies?"

She gets angry. "They're very, very valuable! What are you kidding me?"

I make soothing noises.

"They were films that were going to always be forever."

Reb Sawitz leans back behind his scarred old desk, a fifty-something ex-Hell's Angel with aviator glasses and a Chihuahua trembling in his arm. "First off, I don't believe the coroner," he says. "Second off, when I called the police and told them to speak to me, they didn't call me back. So I called them back. I went down and asked them if they would tell the detective if he wouldn't come up or see me or call me. He still has not. I've had Channel 11, 13, 7, and the *Times*. But not him. And I've known Hal thirty-five years."

He leans back in his chair. "You tell me that he went and saw a doctor that nobody knows—that nobody could find—who told him he had two weeks to live? They didn't find the bird either."

Back in the 1960s, Reb had worked at a collection agency just down the block from Hal's place. They would see each other regularly, dropping in, talking business, trading clients, but Hal was funny because he never talked about personal things. Like his company was called CHN International, and Reb once asked him what CHN stood for, and he said "nothing." Like everyone who knows Hal, he mentions the hair, "dyed black, really pitch black." He'd come in at eight and stay till eleven, take off for lunch and be back open from two to five, and then he would leave, and nobody ever saw him. Nobody ever saw him eat lunch either, or dinner. Reb shakes his head. Hal was a straight shooter, a guy you could count on, a good man, but he was into his bird and his studio and who knows what else. "I think he lived over by the 118 freeway."

Which brings Reb back around to the main mystery: the missing bird. The cops found his car on Martel, found his safe open in the middle of the day. It must have been a robbery. Hal had pictures of Marilyn Monroe that had never been seen, he says. And who knows what else? Which reminds him, he knows a model who said something about jewels; gems or jewelry he had in the safe. She would hang out at his office almost every day, an Asian girl named Caroline who dyed her hair blond—which just between us was definitely the right color for her. He finds her number and dials it on speakerphone. "I have somebody sitting here who's doing a story about Hal," he says and makes a date for me to meet Caroline in person.

"I know this is going to sound like an alibi," Trisha Brown says, "but I was out of the country." Then she laughs and invites me up to her house for dinner. It's a cozy little wooden cottage at the head of old Topanga Road, in a pocket development called Eden Ranch. She's in her forties, shortish and blondish and fearsome with a spoon in the hollandaise sauce. Standing in the kitchen, she tells me that she's the daughter of an FBI agent and a debutante, she went to Harvard, and worked on a thesis on John Barth (because he wrote about people in "bizarre, transitional periods of their life"), then dropped out to work as a stripper and "traipse round" from Alaska to South America. In 1985 she ended up in Hal's office and went in the back and took off her clothes. Hal always took pictures for the book, that was the routine. "But I said, 'I want to be this nice talent, you know? I won't do spreads. And I won't do any manual.' But he actually booked me on some things! He'd give me to Allen Funt, for *Candid Camera*."

After a few years, she realized she really wanted to direct, and then someone asked her to make some wrestling movies. She couldn't believe anybody would want them, but he told her she'd be surprised, and surprised she was—business was so good she went back to Hal, this time as an employer. It was a great relationship. Hal looked out for the lambs. He was never the guy who wanted you to "demonstrate your talents in the field you'll be performing in." She used to take her kid in there.

Sitting around the dinner table, Trisha and her husband serve out the steaks and potatoes and every so often, when the conversation gets too salty, Trisha covers her nine-year-old daughter's ears with her hands. I ask them to explain their business, and David answers as if he's at a trade fair. "The premise is two women wrestle and the friction of breast on breast and crotch on crotch is so stimulating and the anger and hatred and the will to dominate the other person gets them turned on, so one forces the other to have an orgasm against her will."

"And they have to wear little short shorts," says Trisha.

"That say 'Everlast' across the belly."

"Really? It's that specific?"

"Got to," David says. "And they have the boxing gloves. Real boxing gloves. And they never take the gloves off."

Hal started as a girlie photographer in the 1950s up in San Francisco and moved into the cheesecake talent business in the 1960s. When hardcore porn took over and all the other agents in the business went that route, Hal stubbornly stayed out of it, carving out a niche in fetish films and drive-in movies, a niche he called "pretty girl" work. Right here in the catfight world alone there are over a hundred companies, and the Browns alone have made over two hundred videos. They have two kids and a monkey and drive an hour each day to cart their youngest to a better school. "See, we're not big time," Trisha says. "We're people who make a living, you know? They don't hear about this when they talk about showbiz and Hollywood. It's supposed to be, I don't know, somehow bigger than this. You don't think of it as being quite so domestic. We live like regular people. I edit here in the house, answer phones. And Hal was connected to that middle ground, you know? He was the Hollywood nobody knows."

"He wasn't a saint, but if you said, 'I won't go there,' he wouldn't make you go there, whereas with other people, you'd show up and ther"d be the dogs and the ponies and the snakes and you'd be goin' like, 'Euhhhhhh, Momma told me not to come.' "

Her daughter perks up. "There's a song that's called 'Momma Told Me Not to Come.' "

"You're kidding! Really?"

"It's my favorite s-o-n-g."

Trisha suggests I talk to a model named Stacy Burke. She seems to know the most about Hal's death.

Stacy Burke comes down the third-floor balcony of the Hollywood Best Western hotel, a pretty blonde with a beauty mark on her right cheek and an *I Dream of Jeannie* ponytail. She's pulling a rolling suitcase stuffed with stockings, garters, corsets, shoes, and assorted other feminine implements, plus one tuna fish sandwich. She stops outside the hotel room door. "If it was a suicide, then where is his girlfriend? How come she's not around, you know, going, 'Oh my god, what happened?' Why does she just suddenly disappear?"

Then there's his house. The cops can't find it. How is that possible? "It'd have to be, you know, listed somewhere."

And his car. It was parked around the corner instead of behind the building in his private spot.

And the bird.

"If it was a suicide," Stacy says, "he would have made sure his bird was safe. Anyone that's an animal lover knows how that is, and I know how Hal was toward the bird."

Right after they found Hal's body, she talked to the cops. She told them that Hal was not the kind of guy who would burn down his own place. He wouldn't risk other people like that. He was the last of the good guys, always dressed in those old-man kind of slacks with the belt up to here and a white button-down shirt with an undershirt. Hair dyed red, no roots showing hardly ever. He always had Tic Tacs. His nails were always clean. And he never came on to any of the girls, never ever. She went on the web and asked tons of questions because every pretty girl in Hollywood has a website now, and when answers came in she'd tell the cops. That's how she got hooked up with Carol, the C in CHN. Hal left her the business and even she's stumped by what's happened. "We gotta find the person for justice alone," Stacy says. But if there is a murderer, "he's one of us, probably. This person that did this could be amongst us. I mean, he could be a client. He could be a model. You know? There are so many suspects."

Inside the hotel room, the curtains are pulled, and the bed is pushed against the wall to make room for a red wrestling mat. A slouchy cameraman fiddles with lights as the producer introduces himself, giving me his website address and a little background: New York City schoolteacher, fifth grade, fired when they found out about his bondage hobby. He's short, balding, friendly. "Of course I knew Hal. Everybody knew Hal. Hey, Tasha, you worked for Hal, right?"

Tasha's on the crew. She has one of those impossible lean-but-large-breasted bodies and a long cowgirl face. She says she went to Hal when she was eighteen, and he was a fabulous guy, very honest and decent. He sent her out on a lot of shower scenes and body double-type stuff, like making out in a car. "I kind of specialized in that in those days." Another woman says she shot tons of fetish stuff at Hal's studio, too. "There are like three agents," she explains. There's the porn guy, the fetish guy, and Hal. "Hal is the guy you go to if you don't want to do any of that stuff. And I shot at his warehouse a lot." She says she loved him and gives her real name, Candy Fleman, F-l-e-m-a-n, like she's making a point.

Someone says they heard he had cancer.

"I heard he had it for years, and it was in remission."

"He was very meticulous," Tasha says. "He used to count every penny. He was always on time."

"He said that he used to, on his lunch break, go to Fox Studios and consult about lighting issues."

And the parrot—oh god, that parrot.

"We'd be shooting, and the bird would be sitting there. And the director would say 'Action,' and like five minutes later the bird would say, 'Cut!' And everyone's like, 'Who said that?' "

Everyone laughs. As they start stripping down to lingerie, Candy helps set up the lights. "I'm already sore," she says. "I got spanked yesterday."

The photographer perks up. "Why?" he asks. "Were you a bad girl?"

She laughs. "For money," she says.

"And he'd go in the changing room. And he'd whistle. And we're like looking around, 'Oh, it's Max again.' "

"That's the first thing, all of us go, 'Ah! Where's the bird?' "

"Maybe the bird knows the answer."

Russ Meyer sits on his patio overlooking Lake Hollywood with his shirt opening on his big hairy belly. He launches into a story about finding a perfect location to photograph an "overbuilt woman" and then inserting her into that perfect location "in such a way that she would lean out the window, and shake her bagangas, which by and large are large." I haven't got the faintest idea what he's talking about and ask him to tell me about Hal Guthu.

"You guys worked together up in San Francisco?"

"It's not a tremendous remembrance. If you're asking me to recommend him, the best thing you should do is just recommend me." He laughs.

That's when I realize something's wrong with Meyer. He wasn't anything like this the last time I saw him. "Hal was a cameraman," I prod. "I heard that he was the cameraman on *The Immoral Mr. Tease*."

"Was he the cameraman on *Mr. Tease*? I don't think so. Maybe I let him load the film."

"He started a little agency, CHN."

"I wouldn't think much of someone starting a little agency," Meyer says. "Most of these people are trying to get laid themselves, and not having enough push to get women that are overbuilt."

"Excuse me?"

"Overbuilt women! That's why I made a success. Overbuilt women!" Then the phone rings and Meyer picks it up and laughs boisterously, *haw haw haw*, the old operator putting on the schmooze. "Yeah, I'm ready to make pictures," he says, "soon as I find an overbuilt woman. That's what I need. I need an overbuilt woman!"

Caroline's hair is cut short and spiky with the black roots showing, and she's a master of the breathy, giggly, oddly vacant Asian courtesan style—someone said she was like a blonde anyway, so she just decided to go blond and go blond she did. She walked into Hal's office in July of '99, and ever since then she's been coming to his office every day from two to four and just, like, hanging out. "I had a lot of energy, and he had a lot of energy, and we got along," she says. "And he was like my psychic reader because he would tell me things like 'You're gonna make it so good,' and 'Try everything, you never know who you're gonna meet.' And I'd hang on to every word of it. I don't know if he says that to every single girl. It feels like he's saying it just to me." Hal would give her a hundred bucks to buy some clothes, she says. He wore custom shoes because one foot was smaller than the other, from a plane crash when he was young. He told her he had three wives. He would bring out all his old photos, and sometimes he would talk about his kids. "I just wish he wouldn't have to dye his hair—so red. That particular shade of red."

She's pretty sure someone killed him. He would close the car in the back and lock the gate, every time. So why is his car parked in the street? And he would talk about his girlfriend and sometimes the girlfriend would call when he was there, so that was definite. Plus, there was some jewelry. "He showed it to me," she says.

"He showed you jewelry?"

"Yeah, jade and diamond ring," she says. "Yeah. Gold ring. Rubies. All inside the safe. And I called the cops and asked them if they have it, and they said, 'We don't have it.' "

Bill Margold's apartment is just off Sunset Boulevard, a dark little place with a fraying brown carpet and stuffed bears everywhere and football trophies and stacks of old newspapers with articles he wrote and a whole bookshelf filled with videos of his old movies. He stops at the poster of *Disco Dolls*. "That's probably my favorite," he says. "I get my dick bit off at the end and spit out into the audience. I take a stake and skewer a woman. I kill another woman, sodomizing her while I'm drowning her in a vat of chicken soup."

Margold would send Hal the girls who didn't want to do hardcore, and Hal would get them work on pretend-Hollywood movies where they'd barely get scale, and they'd feel better. Margold has a soft spot for Hal because he was nice to Viper, the love of his life. People snubbed her when she first came into town—she would do anything, even double anal, and the other women freaked and wouldn't work with her, but Hal got her work in the fetish world and gave her a home and kept her going. "I think Hal liked her because she was such a battered puppy, and Hal was a kindly man," Margold says. And Hal got her the part she played in *Vice Academy* as the bombshell in the purple dress who teaches the course on sexology, which was perfect for her because she was so wise—she used to say that men were rabbits and women were snakes and that she went into the porn business because then she could have sex with ten thousand men instead of just one, stuff like that. But unfortunately, she also had a bad drug habit and ended up frying herself down to eighty-five pounds, and in February '91 she went naked down Santa Monica Boulevard and got put in Thalians. And then disappeared into America. Last year a magazine writer went looking for her and turned up nothing, just her ID card left on a gravestone out in one of those states.

Bill is fifty-six years old and well over six feet, with a scrappy mustache and a basketball gut. He will tell you that the five most important letters in an adult performer's makeup are r-e-b-e-l and that "the real last American outlaws were the hardcore performers of the 1970s" and that the thing an adult performer wants more than anything else is a hug.

He knocks on the door of his extra bedroom and introduces me to a skinny young brunette from Germany, the latest in a series of unsettled young women he calls his kids. Small and soft-spoken, Marlene tells me she met Hal eight or nine weeks ago, and he was kind of like old Hollywood, taking her in the back to shoot a naked Polaroid. But he seemed nice enough, and he sent her out on one job. Funny thing is, it was a hardcore job. Which didn't bother her so much—she hands me a cassette with her face on the cover, eyes wide and mouth stuffed—but the guy was totally amateur. "He didn't know what to do, like how to hold the camera and how to shoot."

Later, Margold says this was an example of Hal's decline. "I think Hal had settled into his dotage, and finally didn't care."

As I get ready to leave, Margold combs through his book for helpful phone numbers while simultaneously stuffing my hands with porn goodies. We shake hands and he frowns. "The question that nags me is, 'Where's the parrot?' " he says.

"That's what everyone says."

"Sure. Where's the parrot?"

Bob is certain it was murder, he tells me as we tour the industrial park where he runs his bondage empire. Twenty years ago, he and his wife were New York City schoolteachers with an interest in bondage. Then computers came out and Bob started a bondage newsletter and overnight he had four hundred subscribers. But that brought heat from the city, and he ended up escaping to Hollywood like so many others before him. Now he runs his bondage empire out of an industrial park south of LAX with a warehouse and a series of offices and a soundstage across the alley where all of the sets were designed by a top Hollywood set designer. "That is a dungeon," he says, taking me on the tour. "If you come over this way, this is a jail cell. And you may notice some of the details—there's an actual floor. And we even have a drain. We can keep a girl in here for hours."

"And you have a rack."

"Of course. What self-respecting sadist would not have a rack?"

Bob is in his sixties now, with a gray beard and white hair and the rumpled self-regard of a self-made man who has spent his life sitting around one office or another, pushing things along. He says that it's going to sound funny, but even though you're surrounded by beauty and gorgeous women and you have two live-in slaves, after a while it's the product that you worry about. "That's my legacy. I mean, the name B&D Pleasures and Bondage-dot-org have a reputation that I know is going to live on long after I'm gone."

When I mention Hal, he's off, saying that Hal was an amazing guy and the oddest of ducks and never had lunch or hung out and always closed his office from eleven in the morning to two in the afternoon. And he had a parrot that would eat Polaroid photographs, "but only black-and-white Polaroid photographs—a very discerning bird." He was proud of his movie past and showed off books where he was mentioned, kept excellent records and expected commissions promptly, took pride in his dungeon but always thought the bondage stuff was kind of kooky. "I do know that I've been told that some of the girls were sexual companions of his. And I have been told—once again, that's a rumor—that he provided women for sexual purposes, as well as photographic purposes, to some very big names in Hollywood.

"The question remains, who has it in for him? The latest theory is that there was somebody who was actively trying to steal Hal's girls. And allegedly this person said to Hal, 'I'm gonna put you out of business and put you under.' "

I ask him who this person is.

"Let's go into my office," he says.

We cross over to the production building. Sitting on a sofa, he dials the phone and gets a man I'll call Mark. They haggle for a few minutes. "I mean, he's an honest-to-god reporter, and you say, 'This is not for attribution,' he will not put a name with it. But he would like to try to investigate it, and I think that maybe the memory of Hal might deserve that."

Then he hands me the phone. The voice on the other end is blustery, confident. He says he's been in the business twenty years and Hal trained him, taught him everything, and that's why he's talking to me now. "There's a guy who's been a competitor of Hal's who's been out to put him out of business," he says. "His name's Cam Smith. He's been around a year and a half, his girlfriend signed with Hal, and he'd follow her to all her shoots and try to sign Hal's girls.

Hal told me the guy was double-dipping, taking money from girls. He reported it to the State Labor Board. He told me so, in July or September. In my opinion, that's the guy."

Cam Smith is on the phone when I get there and waves me in, still talking. "She's been a little flaky lately, but she just did great today on *Hot Bodies*. And she's fired up to work, definitely." Spread out in neat rows across the beige wall-to-wall carpet of his small Hollywood apartment are rows and rows of naked pictures of pretty girls.

Cam is a good-looking Midwest kind of guy, sandy hair and an earnest face. He was a UPS driver in Iowa when he met his wife at a bar, and she was beautiful and he was just friendly with her at first, and later they fell in love and she wanted to be a model so they moved to Chicago. She got some work, but then they made the big move out to L.A., put all their stuff in storage and drove out and got a hotel room and a manual on how to find an agent. Jobs trickled in, and he did the dirty work, the phone calls and negotiations and driving and coordinating, and six months later they were still struggling when someone slipped him Hal's number. Tracy's career began to take off. For the next eighteen months, Cam talked to Hal regularly about jobs and billings. He says the same things about Hal that everybody says, that you could trust him and that he took the side of his models. Then Tracy left him, and Cam went into a tailspin, drank himself almost to death and ended up in the hospital back in Iowa. "Then I made the big decision—I'll quit drinking. I'll go back to L.A. I'll represent talent."

I ask him how he's finding the girls.

"Word of mouth," he says.

"Are they hard to find?"

"No. I've got more girls in the pipeline than I can get to right now."

Is it true he had a clash with Hal over client-poaching?

"What happened was, Hal and I knew a lot of the same people, some of them were people that I had met through Hal. So he understandably had a right to be upset about that." Then he qualifies the denial. "But some of his girls, a lot of his girls, would come to me and say, 'Look, we love Hal, but the guy hasn't got me a job in four months, and I need the work.' "

"Did he file some kind of complaint against you at the Labor Board or anything like that?"

"May have."

"Really?"

"He may have. I don't know that for a fact, but I had a person who was in town from the East Coast who had gone to see Hal, and what Hal didn't realize was that this person had also been in contact with me, and I found out from this person that Hal had said that I was under investigation by the FBI."

"Really?"

"And that the LAPD was looking into me. And some stuff that was really outlandish."

"So ... you didn't like get pissed off and go down and kill him or anything, did you?"

"No," he says, and laughs. "No, I didn't."

Finally I meet up with Carol Hargraves, the C in CHN. She lives an hour south of Los Angeles in the kind of upscale beach town with million-dollar ranch houses and housewives who look like aging actresses. She's waiting for me at an oceanfront coffee shop, and she's elegant with tossed red hair and a black velvet dress and one of those baggy thick sweaters that hangs around the neck like a shar-pei. She has a tiny diamond stud in her nose. "There are so many stories," she says. "Everybody wants to romance this. In fact, one of the big speculations at first was that it was a land grab—somebody wanted the building from him. But he didn't own the building."

Carol met Hal in 1965, when she was twenty years old and a sportswear buyer at Bullock's. Hal was mostly a photographer and cameraman then, an attractive forty-two-year-old man who seemed very kind and protective. He helped her put together a fashion model portfolio, and they became lovers. They lived together in Hollywood and had two matching black Lincoln Continentals that he kept spotless. They both loved exotic animals, and his first gift to her was a gibbon, "the smallest of the great apes." They found a snake in the desert and added that to their menagerie, then a great horned owl, two Malaysian clawless otters, and some "incidental lizards." One day they decided to expand the operation into a talent agency. The N in CHN was their other partner, a young guy from Brooklyn named Nick, a wannabe photographer who disappeared after a few months and turned up dead from a gunshot in Vegas in '89.

She knew that Hal came from a very religious family in Oregon, that he had been a photographer up in San Francisco, that he was married back in the 1950s but never had any kids of his own. And he had original pictures of Marilyn Monroe. Beyond that he was incredibly private. Mostly they drove out to the desert or to San Francisco and San Diego, hitting flea markets and antique stores to stock up his prop rooms. He never socialized and had no close friends. They hadn't even owned a telephone.

What about his hair? Red or black?

"He had dark brown hair."

"Did he dye it?"

"He had—a solid ego. He kept his body weight down. You could always count on his clean shirt—white shirt—with the top two buttons open. Always."

"Did he have cancer?"

"Eight years ago, he told me he had a growth in the back of his neck. That was as much explanation as I got."

And the girls, did he truly care for them? Was he the grandfather he seemed to be?

"I'm trying to put into some sense of order how he really felt about the models, and the business," she says. "And it's really hard, because he—he had disregard for most people? He did not have disregard, but he did not have a lot of regard? And I think he saw it strictly as a business, in that, for those girls that wanted to do it, it was okay. I think he was emotionally removed."

Hal kept a distance from her, too. Any time she got too close, the wall came down. He used to tell her that she was looking to him as a father figure. He wouldn't even let her take a picture of him, always said the same thing—he was behind the camera, not in front of it.

The only thing she can figure is that it was because of his deformity.

"His legs?"

"Yes," she says. "They were crushed in an airplane accident."

Then she stops. That's not really true, she says. Actually, it was a common birth defect. She doesn't want to use the actual word out of respect for him. "He used to say it was a plane crash, because he was ashamed."

I ask her straight out, what's her opinion: Murder or suicide?

"You know, there are so many unanswered questions ... the car being one of them. The safe was opened and empty. All his books were burned. The woman he was dating. He had shoots set up for Monday. He was to meet with my son on Tuesday, and he was going to teach him about lighting." She goes on: He didn't like guns and smoke, and would a guy who ate the same breakfast cereal every morning for thirty years be the kind of guy who took himself out in a blaze of destruction?

And then there's the bird. When he thought he had cancer, he asked her to take care of Max if he died.

"What about the suicide note?"

"To me it didn't sound like Hal. It didn't sound the way he would speak. Hal was not a whiner, and the note was very whiny. That he had cancer and got to the point where he had a very short time to live. He didn't say anything about Max. So I find it difficult to believe that he wrote that. To me, it looked like somebody was trying to copy his handwriting."

"What about the girlfriend? Is it possible that it's like the plane crash, he's giving himself a girlfriend he doesn't really have?"

"That's possible."

She says that Hal started changing about two years ago, he was getting older, he was in bad health. "He was becoming a sweet old man, that told a lot of sweet old stories. And I think some of them were about himself."

That's why she can't be sure. Maybe he just reached a point where the pain was too much, and he had to control it somehow. "He had controlled his life, all his life. He did things his way. So possibly it was his way of saying, 'I'm out of here, and I'm takin' all my stuff with me.' "

Now dim the lights, please. Put a little theremin on the soundtrack. And here's Hal Guthu himself, alive and well and sitting behind his desk in his storefront office just as he has five days a week for the last thirty years. He'll be dead in nine months, but for now he's still a natty little man with black-framed glasses and a white shirt, the type who takes his time and does things right and takes satisfaction in it. Is he surprised that I don't have a business card? Not a bit. He slips a piece of paper across the desk and tells me to write out my name and address. A big parrot stands on the edge of the desk, clicking its toenails on the tattered wood. I slide the card back, and Hal takes out the famous books, big black ring binders filled with pictures of pretty girls who are naked or almost naked, four or five poses to a page. I sit there flipping pages and whenever I pause, Hal supplies a comment. "I'll be honest with you, she's ugly as hell in person." Or "She won't do open leg." I ask him why he's so adamant about not doing hardcore, and this is what he says: "I have a philosophy about that. I'll degrade women up to a point, and no more."

On the flip side, Hal seems to have very little respect for models who won't do nudity at all. "They're afraid it will hurt their career," he says dismissively. "I tell them every star in the world has done it."

Hal transforms when the phone rings. "You're working?" he says, a big grin on his face. "Oh, you sweetheart, that's terrific!"

It's an ex-model calling to say she landed on her feet. He writes down her number and tells her to keep in touch.

A few days after my interview with Carol Hargraves, the cops find the bird dead of smoke inhalation in the prop room and file Hal's death away as a suicide. But nobody is convinced by this explanation. They keep on whispering about the Russian mafia and the Lost Pictures of Marilyn and stolen jewels and jealous boyfriends, insisting the murder will never be solved. After all, the cops still can't find his house, and the girlfriend never turned up. "Hollywood is full of these mysterious deaths and mysterious doings," says one old rival. "It's almost like the stories that you try to tell somehow come true." He says it with a certain relish.

A few weeks later, forty of Hal's friends gather in Griffith Park in front of an old zoo habitat, showgirls and old Hollywood sports in Gucci loafers and solitary photographers of the kind who have extensive collections of vintage glamour photography. It's peaceful and cool here among the piebald eucalyptus trees. The freeway hum feels almost meditative. There's a sign-up sheet for models who want to carry on Hal's work, and a man with a hundred live doves in white wicker boxes. A leg fetish videographer named Bob is saying that it doesn't mean anything, that the safe was always open. "He kept props in there, like costume jewelry, that's all." Stacy Burke says hi to Caroline Koh.

"Do I know you?" Caroline asks.

"Don't you remember?" Stacy answers. "We did that bondage video together. In the cage." Someone else says that maybe suicide was Hal's way of adding a cloud of mystery, of grasping a bit of immortality. "He did have the devil in his spirit. He loved a good joke. And maybe it was his way of just kind of thumbing his nose. Getting the last laugh. And people would never know for sure."

Then a man hands out candles, and a succession of friends and colleagues tell stories about Hal. When the words are all said, a young woman sings a pretty song about finding peace with the angels and a man opens the wicker boxes and the doves fly straight out over our heads, wings whirring in blurry white circles, urgent and strong, beating hard for home.

As the crowd breaks up, Mark, the man who anonymously fingered Cam Smith as Hal's murderer, falls in with Caroline, the blond Asian. "I've been in production lately," he says, "but now with Hal gone, I've gotta go back into the modeling business full-time."

She asks, "Is it hardcore?"

"No hardcore," he says, "just the way Hal trained me twenty years ago."

Video Bob lingers with Stacy Burke, talking intently about something that involves high heels and seamed stockings. "Think about what you want," he says.

Her answer gets lost in the freeway noise.

EL GRINGO LOCO

Before he started selling drugs for the Sinaloa Cartel, he was an athletic kid from a prosperous American family. He went to college on a football scholarship, found work as a high school football coach. Now he's living at his mother's house in Oregon, working a straight job, bored to death, trying to sort out his feelings. Should he go straight? Should he go back to the cartel? ***You get burned if you stand by the fire***, he says, ***but who wants to be cold?***

The mirror crashes to the floor, and Rigo is in the doorway with his nine in his hand. "We're at war! We're at war!"

The gringo bolts from his bed. He's been in the cartel seven months, a college-educated American kid from the suburbs of Portland with a shaved head and the massive shoulders of the offensive tackle he once was. It started out pure fun, easy money, gorgeous women, and the camaraderie of soldiers. They called him La Flama Blanca, the white flame, which somehow inspired a series of *Talladega Nights* jokes. *We know how to shake and bake Flama Blanca style!* And man, did they party. But lately the gringo's been getting paranoid. That's why he put the mirror against his door, the only alarm system that still works after Rigo freaked out and smashed all the alarms, thinking they were spy cameras.

"We're at war!" Rigo shouts again.

As usual, Rigo's out of his mind on coke and ecstasy and massive quantities of booze. He's thirty, skinny and good-looking, with the vagued-out sweetness of someone nursing many inner wounds. His uncle gave him a job cleaning meth when he was thirteen. When he was fifteen he watched his grandfather stab a man to death. When he was eighteen he stabbed a man and then spent five years in prison. In the past few months he's become the gringo's best friend.

"Calm down," the gringo says. "Tell me what happened."

What happened is Rigo went to the projects to score coke and some guy sold him a $10 bag that seemed light, so they had words and Rigo punched him in the face. According to the narco code, the guy is going to have to come back hard. The alternatives are ostracism or death.

"They're coming for us," Rigo says. "We're fucking at war right now."

Then Rigo sits down on his bed and starts to pass out. Thinking there's a gang of killers on the way, the gringo says, "Motherfucker, what the fuck?"

Rigo wakes up for a second. "I just need some milk and cookies, Mom."

After that, nothing will rouse him. So the gringo takes his gun and stands watch all night, hoping this nightmare will dissipate in the light of morning.

No such luck. In the light of morning, Rigo still wants to kill the guy. He calls his cousin Demente, a hit man who shows up with an extra Glock. Rigo says, "I'll talk to the guy, but I'll probably shoot him." And Demente holds out the gun to the gringo.

This is it, the point of no return. If the gringo doesn't take the gun, his brief, improbable career as a white American in a Mexican cartel is over.

"Let's do it," he says.

The gringo from Portland is going to war.

Before he went to Mexico, the gringo was an athletic kid from a prosperous American family with two beach houses. Life was good until he was eleven, when his parents divorced and his mother married a much younger man, leaving the gringo with a fatherless ache that lasted all through his teen years. But he poured his energy into sports and never took illegal drugs till he was twenty-three. He made All State in high school and got a football scholarship to

Portland State, where he picked up a bachelor's degree in communication and a painkiller habit. His biggest rebellion was a taste for Latin American revolutionary history. After college he found work as a high school football coach.

He's telling this story at his mother's house in Portland. He's been back from Mexico for two and a half months, found a job doing telemarketing from a sterile cubicle and taking shit from a snotty boss, and he's trying to sort out his feelings. Should he go straight? Should he go back to the cartel? "You get burned if you stand by the fire," he says, "but who wants to be cold?"

His dilemma began soon after he graduated from college, when he started selling painkillers to pay for his habit. He started to think of himself as an "illegalist," his term for a revolutionary without a revolution. He read Mao and Castro and Chomsky and Kropotkin, cultivating "a rage against a society that is created to keep us from thought and from being happy."

Three years later everything fell apart. "One of my friends is in a mental institution, one got addicted to heroin, and I introduced them to pills." He felt so bad, he stopped caring if he lived or died and did reckless things that attracted the attention of the police. So when his mom saw an ad for English teachers in Guadalajara, he jumped at the chance to escape. Emiliano Zapata! Pancho Villa! What better place to clean up than sunny Mexico?

He arrived in October and got a job teaching English at a factory, waking up at 6:30 and catching the train, a period he now thinks of as "the time I was trying to pretend to be a normal person." But one night, he and another teacher were in a club, and a guy came up with a tray of free beer, said he was a hit man from Michoacán who had decided to protect them—and lifted his shirt to flash his gun. The gringo was fascinated. In the circles he was running in, narcos were Robin Hoods who battled the corrupt government and refused to abide by social norms. Ballads memorialized narcos' deaths. What could be cooler?

That November, the same teacher took him to a party in a big house on a tree-lined street near the Expo Guadalajara. The host was a skinny young guy who spoke perfect English. Call me Rigo, he said, launching into the fantastic story of his life as a fourth-generation narco. One of his first memories was his dad kicking a hole in the wall and digging out two cases of money and a shotgun. He was eight. Next time they met, he was sixteen and his dad gave him an ounce of cocaine for a Christmas present.

Another night in another club, one of the gringo's friends bought some ecstasy from a guy whose boss then came up to their table. He was in his thirties, a good-looking, relaxed dude, six feet tall, big for a Mexican, with the Buddha belly of a man who loves to drink and party. "Call me Cuz," he said.

Cuz and the gringo hit it off. Cuz was funny, an outgoing party guy everybody instantly liked. He grew up in Juárez and loved Americans, was a huge music fan and rave promoter. Soon they were exchanging stories about their backgrounds, and it was amazing because they were both the black sheep of wealthy families with elder brothers who were the favorite. They both loved *Scarface* and *Pulp Fiction* and *American Gangster*. They talked about the bad things they had done and the lives they were destined to live. "You can correct yourself all you want," Cuz said, "but you're still going to be that person, the person you are."

That night, Cuz made out like he was a little guy who sold a few pills at raves. "You hang out with these teachers; you could sell to these teachers," he said, giving the gringo half an X to try. "Remember, call me tomorrow. Don't forget."

The gringo did as he was told.

A week later, Cuz called back. "Let's get some beers and go to this little party." So they gathered some of the gringo's friends and hopped in a cab and drove till they were forty miles out of town and starting to get nervous. Suddenly, at the top of a hill, a squad of *federales* appeared. They searched everybody but Cuz, who walked right past them as if he were invisible. The gringo and his friends followed him over a ridge onto a mountaintop lit up like a nightclub with five thousand people dancing. A line of gunmen in ski masks stood guard around the perimeter with AR-15s. The gringo turned to Cuz. "Are those more *federales?*"

"No, those are our dudes."

The gringo was starting to realize that Cuz was connected in a big way. He walked from one hug and high five to the next. He seemed to know everybody. He led the gringo to a tent with heat lamps and black leather couches and beautiful women who all seemed to be wearing big fat gold men's watches—the sign of a narco princess, as the gringo would soon learn. "You see one of those watches on a girl, you steer clear."

They were in the narco tent. Famous DJs from Europe chatted nervously with the gangsters, who tended to fall into categories denoted by the drugs they sold—the coke guys were the scariest, dancing like maniacs and giving you that cold coke stare. But the gringo was oblivious, bopping up to the most dangerous guys and babbling like a goofball. He had a way of twisting his face into comic expressions that contradicted his football body and made him hard to pigeonhole: Was he a thug or an idiot? Not always in a friendly way, the narcos asked, "Who is this guy?"

Cuz wanted them all to take acid. The gringo had never done hallucinogens before but found it hard to say no. Cuz just laughed at everything. There was no darkness in him, no judgment. Nothing was true, so everything was permitted, as the old Russian anarchists used to say. Fuck it, the Gringo said. "Let's do it." So the sun came up as the acid came on, and they were in this beautiful Mexican countryside where everything seemed to fall into place and Cuz seemed like a prophet. The world was divided into good and evil and light and dark, he said, but all divisions were profitable to somebody, and it was the same with the cartels dividing the world into families, raising prices in collusion with the cartel of the U.S. government. But some day the world would be one, and all the countries and cartels would go away. That's why Cuz didn't use hit men or deal heroin or speed or crack, because that ruined people's lives. If it was his destiny to be a criminal, he could at least improve his karma by sticking to softer drugs.

"If we're dealing coke to a girl," he said, "what will she do? Break into her parents' room and steal money out of her dad's wallet. If she's on X, she sneaks into her dad's room to give him a hug."

Oh, how they laughed! In the gringo's mind, it all made perfect sense, as if his whole life had been leading up to this moment. Stuck between being a bad son and a good son, he could make up for the sins of selling those horrible painkillers and getting his friends addicted and still follow his illegalist destiny. He could have a stretch of lawlessness in a place where lawlessness still exists. In his addled mind, it was a strange kind of self-improvement program that might finally purge his suicidal impulses. His Che Guevara quote tattoo said it all: *We cannot be sure of having anything to live for unless we're willing to die for it.*

Still, the good son had to teach the next day. So Cuz walked him down to a little mom-and-pop stand to catch the bus back to Guadalajara. While they waited, Cuz turned his wild-eyed grin on the cashier. "I'm on acid right now," he said.

The cashier smiled. "The 1970s are back—nice."

Cuz started him off at a high price, $7 a pill, supplying acid, X, and molly, which is X so pure you can snort it or put it under your tongue. The molly sold for $15 each. The gringo could make $400 in a single night, almost as much as he earned for a whole month of teaching. He also started hanging out with Cuz a couple of days a week, helping him sort and package pills and move money from place to place.

Soon after, his mom came down for the holidays, and Cuz took them out to lunch at a fancy Argentine steak place. She asked, "Is Mexico safe?" Cuz said, "Oh, don't worry; we're just getting rid of all the dirt balls, rapists, and killers to make a better society." They hit it off, even became Facebook friends, and that helped seal the gringo's bond with Cuz, because Mexico is all about family. He didn't tell his mom that eighteen headless bodies had just been found a mile from her hotel.

By January he had stopped teaching altogether. He worked parties and gay clubs and hung out with hot French girls. He was their peek into the glamorous narco lifestyle—a dancing bear, as he puts it.

But more and more, he found himself hanging out with Rigo. Talk about an illegalist! Rigo would walk out of a club and shoot his gun in the air. He would fire off a couple of rounds at the front door instead of ringing the doorbell. He had been a meth addict, a heroin addict, a professional killer who took payment in cars. He never judged and never criticized, accepting the craziest behavior with a laugh and a shrug. "I always like having people around who are crazier than I am." More important, he was the dauphin of a powerful cartel family, and as long as he was around, nobody would touch them—as the gringo learned one night when he got into a club dispute with a thug who threatened to slit his throat. He went straight home and called Rigo.

"This fucking guy from Sinaloa threatened to kill me," he said.

"Don't worry," Rigo said. They'd have to get permission to hit a white guy, and his uncle would hear about it. "I'll put the word out; nothing will happen."

And nothing did.

Around March, the Gringo moved in with Rigo. Their housemates included a Satanist death-metal fan who had been arrested for manslaughter, the burned-out son of another powerful family, and a hot-dog salesman who doubled as muscle in dangerous times. There were bullet holes in the palm trees and rumors of bodies buried in the backyard, left by a former owner who led one of the cartels. They called it the House of Pain, and the gringo made it his mission to turn it into the Happy House. To Rigo, he was a minty blast of American optimism.

For the first month, they did a lot of coke. People would come by, drink a beer, buy some pills. Or they'd go to one of the nightclubs Rigo's uncle owned, hanging out in a private lounge with bottles of champagne and Johnnie Walker Black, the narcos' favorite drink. Rigo's uncle would come by with his fancy watch and $300 shoes and give them a big bag of *lavada*, the narco drug of choice, coke double-washed to clean out the chemicals. It had no bite and didn't make you hunger for more, just lifted you up on a waft of soft air and deposited you in a fluffy cloud—and it smelled like strawberries.

Hour after hour Rigo would explain the business. Somebody always runs the plaza, which is sometimes an actual plaza and sometimes just a part of town. Rigo knew how much things cost, how to move things, how things worked in the U.S., and what groups you needed to make alliances with. He taught the gringo how to recognize other narcos, the flashy ones who wore designer sunglasses and glittery shirts and the kind who looked like skate punks. Almost always they carried three phones: one for the boss, one for the customers, and one for the family. And you have to know your history, he said. The narcos get offended when you don't know the history of Mexico or the cartels.

The management of violence had a single rigid rule: If they lay their hands on you, come back tenfold. That's how Rigo's cousin was killed. He set up a meeting between two guys who were fighting, and one of the guys slapped the other guy. The guy who was slapped killed the guy who slapped him and then killed Rigo's cousin just for setting up the meeting. So Rigo and his hit-man cousin Demente had no choice. They burst into the man's home and killed him along with his entire family.

After that, Rigo went out of control. His uncle was dropping off kilos of crystal, and Rigo was such a good cleaner he could save a tenth of the product, which he smoked. He got so paranoid he spent half his time in his room with his gun. He cheated on his wife, and she left with their three kids. Finally, his uncle came to him and said, "You're skinny; you don't look so good. I hate to see you like this. I'm not going to do business with you till you clean up."

Rigo got a job as a bellhop, got fired and got another job and got fired again. And another. And another. Finally, his uncle called and said, "What are you planning on doing?"

"I want to do whatever you want me to do and gain your trust back," Rigo answered.

That's why Rigo was so obsessed with the rules he was always breaking. Under his training, the gringo felt militarized. They were soldiers in a war, brothers in arms, and nothing in his white-bread American life had ever felt so real.

All that winter the gringo continued to work as Cuz's sidekick. Sometimes Cuz would say, "You want to make some money, just drive this down the street." One time he drove fifteen thousand pills to a guy's house. Once, Cuz came out with a black bag the size of a loaf of bread, a million pesos in small bills. Cuz made it all seem like a rolling party, blasting his beats on the car radio. "You hear this part? You hear this part?"

One day Cuz was flipping through a magazine called *Proceso* and he came to a picture of Joaquín "El Chapo" Guzmán, leader of the Sinaloa cartel and a billionaire who has appeared on *Forbes* magazine's list of the world's richest men. He asked, "What do you think about this guy?"

"I don't know what to think," the Gringo said.

"He'll fuck you over, but he has a big heart," Cuz said. "He'll fuck you over if you need to be fucked over."

That was the first hint that the gringo's chain of command ultimately stopped with El Chapo himself. The next hint came from another regular at Rigo's house, a volatile thirty-nine-year-old gangster named Roberto who dated an Argentinean stripper and loved to talk about killing people. "If I was having lunch with your mom," he said with an evil grin, "I would tell her, 'He's with Chapo now.' "

So the gringo was working for the Sinaloa cartel, the most powerful drug-trafficking organization in the world. So be it, he thought. He had come to see everything through the eyes of his friends, whom he loved for their loyalty and straightforward, no-bullshit way of living. The other cartels were the dickheads. Worst of all were Los Zetas, a cartel from southern Mexico that was making a big push on Guadalajara and the north. "They use a lot of poor people to do their shit, guys from the projects, Central American guys, guys who are willing to kill for nothing. Chapo ran the good cartel. He buys things for people and helps with public works projects and stuff." To this day, the gringo always calls Cuz "my boss," and it's hard not to hear an echo of the fatherless son in his voice.

But the sane part of him, the part that wanted to live, started to live in fear. At one of the mountain parties, he saw a guy hit on one of the narco princesses and get dragged out into the night by two big guys, never to be seen again. At another Cuz was in the narco tent, chatting with a former MMA fighter, when the gringo looked too long at his girlfriend and made a joke about his fighting skills. "Are you challenging me?" the MMA fighter asked. The tension lasted all through the long night. And Rigo's house kept getting crazier. One guy named Manuel was so out of control they'd put Xanax in his drink to calm him down. One time he opened the refrigerator and pissed in one of the drawers, so they beat him up and threw him in the street. An hour later he came stumbling back. Rigo said, "I'm sorry I hit you, but you can't piss in the fridge."

Manuel looked confused. "I pissed in the fridge?"

By the night the mirror came crashing down, when Rigo roared his war cry and the gringo made his decision to take the gun, all this seemed almost normal. They prepared for the gunfight by doing coke and listening to heavy metal for ten hours. That made perfect sense too. When they finally got to the projects, it was three in the morning and the gringo was so wired he pissed on a gang sign and shouted, "Come out, motherfuckers. We're here."

The coke dealer appeared with ten buddies. They fanned out behind him as Rigo walked up to the guy, his nine in his back pocket. The Gringo moved his hand over his piece, ready to draw.

For a long moment life and death hung in the balance.

Finally the dealer stepped forward and held out his right hand. "I'm so sorry," he said.

He had discovered who Rigo's uncle was, and he was scared to the point of shaking. That's when the Gringo finally had a flash of sanity. *What the fuck am I doing here? How did I get into this?* But it passed quickly as they left in triumph, Rigo and Demente laughing at the crazy gringo pissing on the gang sign. "El gringo es loco," said Demente—high praise from a guy whose nickname translates as "insane."

As a reward for his service, Rigo revealed his real last name. "From now on, bro, you are family." La Flama Blanca was no longer enough. The crazy white boy from Portland deserved a new name: El Gringo Loco.

All that summer, protected by Rigo's name, El Gringo Loco worked a circuit of three beach towns—Manzanillo, Puerto Vallarta, and

Sayulita. By now he was paying $4 a pill and selling them for $25 each. He quit drinking and cut back on X and even looked into a job selling time-shares at inflated prices but decided it was too dishonest. "You get a pill from me and it's a good pill and you pay the same price everyone is paying. Taking money from people in a fraud, I couldn't fucking do it."

That's the paradox he still can't get over. In Portland he might have done it. But in this world where violence settled disputes, the Bob Dylan rule applied: To live outside the law you must be honest.

But the paranoia got worse. At night his mind would go to the worst thoughts—torture, death, dismemberment, dishonor. One night in Sayulita he was selling in a bar and a guy with a pit bull took him into a back room, where a group of men were waiting for him. The boss pointed a finger at him and pulled an imaginary trigger. "You need to leave—you need to leave now." Another night in Puerto Vallarta a Zeta chieftain cornered him in a restaurant. "I know where your fucking pills come from, man. You shouldn't be working here. This is past your border." Another night he was at a party, and Roberto announced, "This is the boss from the dragonflies. This is the distributor." He was pointing at the gringo. The problem was, dragonflies were a superior brand of X controlled by another cartel. The gringo wasn't supposed to be selling them.

"Shut the fuck up," he told Roberto. "You're going to get me killed."

Roberto gave him the cold eye. "You're lucky you're my friend."

The beautiful girl who gave blow jobs for X was no consolation. To get his mind off his troubles the gringo started to write poetry. "I need to get the crazy out of my life," he thought.

Instead, he moved back into Rigo's house for the three craziest months of his life, partying his way into narco legend.

In November it all came crashing down. Cuz sent him to Mexico City with ten kilos of weed and he came back with 50,000 pesos in his pocket, and no sooner did he arrive back at Rigo's house than he ran into a phalanx of cops. "Hey, gringo, we need to see ID."

A year had passed since he started the narco life. The cops searched him and found the money. "What the fuck is this?" He put on an innocent face. "That's my rent." The cops searched further and found an X. "What the fuck is this?" He said, "Guys, these aren't my jeans". They cuffed him and put him in the car. From the backseat he tried to make a deal. "Take half the money and we call it a day."

No deal.

Still afraid to give his real name, he pretended to be German and demanded a translator. That pissed the cops off so much, they sent him to one of the most notorious prisons in Mexico, Puente Grande. On the bus another prisoner warned him, "Gringo, you better get ready. These guys don't play."

Walking in, he was shaking inside. They put him in a tiny cell with six other men. The showers didn't work; you had to pay for your food, phone calls, weed—that's all they did in prison, smoke weed. He found his way to a neutral area called Beverly Hills and made friends with some cholos, who saved his ass when he got into a fight with another narco. Finally, Rigo called his mom, and his mom found Cuz on Facebook, and they hired a lawyer, who got him transferred to an immigration prison to wait for his papers. It took seventeen days. One day a guy from Honduras brought up the Zetas, and El Gringo Loco couldn't help repeating the Sinaloa line: "Their own mothers don't love them."

"*Yo soy los Zetas*," the Honduran said. After a tense moment, the gringo twisted his face into one of his goofy expressions and cracked a joke. "Oh, but I don't know any from Honduras."

Laughter saved him once again. The next day he was on a plane back to Portland.

Now he's going back to Mexico. It has been ten weeks since he was deported, and he's already sick of his cubicle job. He's sitting in his mother's elegant suburban house, skimming the internet for news about Guadalajara, where a cartel prince called El Changel just got wounded in a gun battle with police, unleashing violence all over western Mexico. Still, he thinks it's a fine time to slip back down for one more taste of the narco life. The complication is, he's bringing a reporter who looks alarmingly like a DEA agent—me. Hopefully his friends won't think he got turned in prison.

The night before he leaves, he sends me this message:

I feel nervous, good and excited, mostly nervous. I mean, I trust my people, but these are killers—if I was not nervous then I suppose I would need to check my pulse. I did not sleep well last night, I have to get my war face on. In the end I am a soldier and I have trained myself for this. I have said good-bye to my friends, and if I go then it has been a hell of a ride. I get to go from being a normal white guy who works a nine-to-five and stands in line at the grocery store to a man who is feared, respected and loved. I look forward to it with an absurd amount of excitement. In the end I would rather die on my feet than live on my knees.

After his plane lands, the gringo meets me in a hotel lobby. "I can't believe I'm back here," he says. "It's definitely not a world I want to come back to."

But he's going to go see Cuz tonight to get some acid and X and do a few little deals. And Rigo is coming over in a few minutes—in fact, there he is now, just as the gringo described him, a skinny, good-looking guy who looks about twenty-five, if twenty-five were as sad as seventy. He's tweaked out on something, fanning his neck and impatient to go see a hostess who used to be a narco wife—yes, she has a gold watch. "A nice one," the Gringo says.

Rigo doesn't care. He's supposed to meet her in eight minutes. No, seven minutes. And man, what an ass she has. "She's sitting on it."

They drain their beers and go.

The scariest part is the anticipation of meeting Cuz for the first time. The cartels *really* don't like journalists—according to the Committee to Protect Journalists, they've beheaded, tortured, and shot at least forty-five of them in the past seven years. Many more have disappeared.

The next afternoon the gringo takes me to Rigo's house. This too is just as he described it, a two-story place on a pretty, tree-lined street. Inside it's just raw walls and a couple of sofas around a glass coffee table, some weights against a wall, a brown lawn out back.

Rigo points out a big hole where a friend shot the wall. The doors have all been kicked in; not a single one closes properly. Out back they show off the bullet holes in the trees.

Odd as it may be, Rigo really does seem like a sweet guy, eager to like and be liked. Maybe that's why he starts telling his backstory, his teen years cleaning meth and the lessons his father taught him: *It's better to have a gun and not use it than to need a gun and not have it*, for example. Each story has sub-stories and punch lines to illustrate the ridiculous glory of narco life. Over and over he insists the narcos are good people and kill only people who need to be killed—except the Zetas, of course.

When we part that night, Rigo pushes a button on his dashboard and then another button to release a secret compartment—in some narco cars you have to tune the radio to a certain station before you push the buttons. Inside is a space that spans the width of the car, big enough for forty kilos. He takes out a bag of X and hands it to the gringo—to El Gringo Loco.

Saturday, Rigo and the gringo head downtown for some 6 peso tacos. Rigo's already on his second or third beer of the day. Every few minutes he spots some hot girl. "Look at that ass. She's sitting on it!" Walking toward the city's big open-air market, they stop for Cuban cigars and some gifts for the Gringo's nieces. At the taco stand Rigo brings up the guy who shot his cousin. "We killed his whole family, just walked into the house and started shooting."

In the same detached voice, he says he killed one of them from about as far away as those poles across the street. "It's not like the movies. You pull the trigger, and he falls down. There's no blood."

How does he carry that around? "No problem," he answers. "I had nightmares for a couple of weeks, but they were about my cousin dying alone in the street. I don't have any remorse."

Cuz calls and the gringo is already laughing by the time he picks up the phone. They make plans to meet at a steakhouse so he can introduce me. Before the gringo hangs up, he asks, "Do you have any wash?" Meaning *lavada*, the double-washed strawberry cocaine of the narcos. "Great, bring me some. Yeah, I got the money."

A few more hours, a few more beers, and it's time to meet the boss. At the steakhouse they get a table in the back and shoot the shit until he shows up—a big guy with a small forehead and a Fred Flintstone jaw darkened by a five-o'clock shadow. His girlfriend is a green-eyed beauty with major cleavage and skintight leatherette pants. After some teasing about Cuz's Polish soccer jersey—"I just bought it to go with my shoes; I didn't even look at the logo"—the gringo asks if he brought the wash. Cuz hands over a little plastic bag filled with white powder, and the gringo turns aside to take a quick snort off the tip of Rigo's ignition key. "Nobody saw me, did they?" Cuz says, "Yes, they saw you." He thinks it's funny.

After lunch we walk out of the restaurant with beers in our hands. A waitress stops us, so we chug down in the doorway and head for the car. Another bump off the ignition key for everyone and we're off, following Cuz's black SUV—leaving the safety of a public place, putting our lives in his hands. Adrenaline mixes with the cocaine, and every nerve is thrumming with a heightened sense of being alive. "There's the club where I shot off the gun," Rigo says. "There's the doorway where my cousin got killed."

Cuz leads us to a house in a suburban neighborhood with a pool and a bunch of attractive people drinking, an oddly domestic scene with a little kid running around the pool and five narcos huddling across the yard. There's a mountain party tonight, and they're partying here until it starts. The narcos slip outside to smoke a little dope, slip into the bathroom to snort the *lavada*. Cuz wants everyone to stay cool so they can make it to the mountain party.

Standing behind his boss, the gringo shakes his head—*Please, God, no*. Cuz always wants to hang out in the narco tent, and you're stuck out there in the middle of nowhere with all those guns—no thanks. But he doesn't say this to his boss.

Cuz doesn't take anything too seriously. His family is so rich, he says, that his older brother, the chosen one, is one of the five biggest landowners in Mexico. When Cuz's father dies, he'll inherit a fortune. So he keeps his business low-key, running the pill market in Guadalajara and on the coast. As long as he sticks to pills and avoids the cocaine and meth other families control, he's all right.

And El Gringo Loco? Why him? Was it his white skin? His brains? His twisted sense of humor?

"He's my little brother," Cuz says.

After a couple of hours the gringo, brimming with relief, says goodbye. Bro hugs all around, plus promises to stay relatively straight and rise at dawn for the second phase of the mountain party—Cuz is a hard guy to say no to.

Now the real party begins. We head downtown to the club district, and man, is it hopping. The streets are jammed with sexy young women tottering by in high heels and short, tight skirts. Rigo leads the way into an American-style bar, and the shaggy young bartender spots the gringo, comes around the bar to greet him with open arms. "Where the fuck have you been?" He gives us free beers and shots and after awhile takes the gringo into the bathroom to do a little deal. The gringo loves the action, it is clear, loves being the American all the Mexicans want to see. He says he's thinking of doing six months in the U.S. and six months down here. "You should come down for spring break," Rigo says. "Yeah, that's when the six months would start."

There's a stubborn core deep in that skinny body of Rigo's that just doesn't give a shit about living. It's oddly endearing. He wants to get healthy and be good but deep down can't believe that he deserves it, so he protects and punishes himself with booze and drugs and lays his neck bare to the knife of existence—which is, when you think about it, pretty much how you'd want a man who has killed fifteen people to feel.

Outside, the Gringo sighs. "You see how he is."

Never mind. The night goes on. Another cerveza. Another snort. The true El Gringo Loco is coming out now, sliding free in the haze of intoxicants. On the great avenue of trees and fountains called Lopez Mateos, there's a street party with a reggae band, and the crowd is like Times Square on New Year's Eve. One of Rigo's girls shows up—very pretty and sweet—and then it's on to a rock club called Barramericano, where a good band is playing the Strokes note for note, then on to his uncle's club with the pretty girl driving.

Here we are at one of the best clubs in Guadalajara. "Do you want to go through the front door or the narco door?" Rigo asks.

The narco door, of course. It's black steel with a little speakeasy barred window and opens wide for Rigo. Everyone's so happy to see him. Inside the club is huge and packed with beautiful women and sharp men and spinning lights and a sound system as fancy and expensive—Rigo says it cost a million bucks—as ones in the best clubs in New York.

Ah, Mexico. El Gringo Loco is in his element now, hitting on the prettiest women. With his massive shoulders and goofy animated face, he is the dancing bear, and you can't help but laugh when he shimmies into yet another gaggle of beautiful women. And now Rigo is hitting on a stunning little thing in a skintight micromini while his date waits at the table. "Dude, you already got a hottie right there!" He laughs. "Yeah, but look at that ass. She's sitting on it!"

This goes on till five in the morning. Then Rigo takes his hottie home and drops another X. "Good times," he says.

Two days later El Gringo Loco flies back to Portland and his telemarketing cubicle. In the morning he writes this note:

For now, I will try the "normal" life and see how it fits. I will try to laugh at the guy who talks shit to me at the club, listen to my boss belittle me in front of my employees and remember this is not Mexico and I can't just call one of my friends to teach him his final lesson. The days of El Gringo Loco are done...

Then, thinking again of Mexico, glorious tragic Mexico, where the women are beautiful and life is sweetened by the presence of death, he adds a final line:

But never say never...

NOT GUILTY BY REASON OF AFGHANISTAN

After the 9/11 terrorist attacks on America, on rare nights he fell asleep, Nathan Powell dreamed of poisonous fogs and people on fire. He stopped taking cabs because he thought the drivers might be terrorists. Then he began producing a film about Afghanistan. And then, not long after, the Afghanistan-born director of the film, Jawed Wassel, was found in a shallow grave, chopped into little pieces.

This much is certain: On the night of October 3 of the year 2001, a man named Nathan Powell brutally killed a man named Jawed Wassel. The causes of death noted by the coroner included two stab wounds in Jawed's back and signs of "blunt force trauma" that included broken facial bones and an "eggshell type" fracture of his skull. The coroner's job was complicated because he was working from fragments. As he stated in his report, speaking in the eternal present tense of dictation, "body parts are received separately and these consist of a torso, a severed head, and dismembered upper and lower extremities." The pieces of Jawed Wassel arrived in various bags and boxes. The torso was in Box 1, Bag A. In Box 2, Bag B, the coroner found "a dismembered lower extremity including upper leg, lower leg, and foot." In Bag D of the same box, he found blood-stained bath towels and socks and a V-neck pullover shirt of the Club Monaco brand, along with a segment of blue hacksaw blade with bone tissue still adhering to the teeth. In this box he also found sponges, paper towels, a Brillo pad, and one bloodstained hand towel "with a Christmas holiday pattern." Jawed's head arrived in a refrigerator drawer. "The bony portion of the neck is transected through the body of the fourth cervical vertebra. The right arm is dismembered by incision of the skin and soft tissues including muscle, tendon, nerve, and blood vessels... Sectioning of the brain reveals typical distribution of gray and white matter and deep cortical structures." These things are true. They are solid. The ventricles of Jawed's brain were not dilated. His cerebellum, pons, medulla, and brain stem were all "unremarkable," which is the word scientists like to use because *normal* is too vague and easy to dispute. His paratracheal soft tissues were unremarkable. The endocardium of his heart was unremarkable. His aorta was unremarkable and his vena cava was unremarkable and his pulmonary vasculature was also unremarkable. And that is all I can tell you that is certain and solid.

This is a story for our time, dark and violent and complicated almost beyond understanding. In one version of the story, the Twin Towers fall and raise a cloud of madness and paranoia that sends Nathan Powell, a man with a young daughter and no criminal record, off on his own personal war on terrorism. He commits an act of senseless murder that makes sense to him, which has both narrow legal implications in terms of his motive and also larger implications in terms of the horror all around us. In the second version, there's little sense and no point in puzzling over it. There's nothing but greed and cunning and a monstrous attempt to use the falling towers to blame the victim, and Jawed Wassel is the first casualty of a phony war. Either way, Nathan Powell has pleaded not guilty by reason of temporary insanity, and the difficult truth behind his terrible crime becomes a warning sign of the world we entered on September 11, 2001.

First, Nathan Powell's version of the story. This is how he has told it to me, to the police, to his lawyer, to several psychologists, and to a polygraph examiner. He's also written it out numerous times. Although some versions are more detailed than others, the essential story has varied little.

In 1996, after a troubled childhood, a couple of failed relationships, and a few stints at studying film at Columbia and Hunter College, Nathan was thirty-three and living in New York when he started working with an Afghan immigrant named Jawed Wassel on a film called *FireDancer*. He was the producer and Jawed was the writer and director, and they split their deal down the middle, fifty-fifty. In 1997, Jawed went to Afghanistan and came back with stories of fighting against the Taliban with the Northern Alliance. Nathan says he saw pictures of Jawed with an AK-47 and also heard Jawed making anti-American declarations—that the U.S. was responsible for the suffering in Afghanistan because Ronald Reagan supported the Afghan rebels against the Soviet Union but then abandoned them, or that the U.S. didn't care about Afghans so much as an oil pipeline through Uzbekistan. But Nathan didn't give it much thought because that kind of talk was typical in artsy circles, and anyway he'd heard the same kind of thing many times from his father, a banjo-playing socialist who worshiped Pete Seeger and Woody Guthrie.

In 1999, Nathan and Jawed went to Washington, D.C., to start shooting their film and immediately ran into many troubles, such as a huge squabble over a line in the script that suggested that one of the characters in the movie might not be a virgin. This led to physical threats and a lot of talk about honor killing, the tribal custom of avenging stains on a family's name with blood. Around that time, the lead actor was replaced with Baktash Zaher, who had trained to be a pilot at a flight school in Florida. And members of a Taliban delegation to Washington stayed at the house of one of the Afghans supporting the production, sharing quarters with a couple of crew members.

In November 2000, Jawed mentioned that his contacts in northern Afghanistan had offered to arrange an interview with Osama bin Laden. When Nathan told another friend about this, the man offered to pose as a journalist and kill bin Laden, so Nathan tried to contact the CIA through an acquaintance named Marc Palmer, who brushed him off.

In June 2001, Nathan and Jawed attended a meeting with another *FireDancer* producer named Kate Wood, and Jawed told them that he was going to Afghanistan to make a documentary and please not to tell anyone where he was going. When he came back six weeks later, he was limping and wouldn't answer any questions.

Then the planes hit the Twin Towers. Nathan had a clear view of the whole thing from the window of his loft just across the East River, sitting there with his wife and their four-year-old daughter. At one point he used binoculars and saw a person jump. Then he talked to Jawed on the phone, and Jawed said America was finally getting a taste of its own medicine.

On TV, Nathan saw pictures of Arabs in Jersey City celebrating the attacks. The next day, he says, he saw some Arabs on his own street pumping their fists and cheering. A few days later, he went to Jawed's house and found Jawed watching the news with Baktash and his sister, Vida Zaher-Khadem, who was Jawed's associate director. When they started glancing at the screen and "whispering among themselves in Farsi," it made him suspicious. What were they hiding? Then Jawed said the CIA must have organized the attacks to provoke a war and bail out the floundering Bush administration.

Later there was a disturbing meeting with Jawed and a man named Eric Rayman, who argued that the movie should say "something positive" about the Taliban. Nathan couldn't believe it. What was going on here? Jawed had always said he opposed the Taliban, but maybe it had all been a horrible lie. And what about Baktash training at that flight school in Florida? *Why didn't Baktash ever actually become a pilot?*

Over the next few weeks, Nathan couldn't sleep or fell into vivid nightmares. He stopped taking cabs because he thought the cabdrivers might be terrorists. He made plans to leave the city, but he didn't tell people because he was afraid they'd think he was crazy.

All through this, Jawed was pushing him to use the attacks to promote *FireDancer*. At first he thought it was a horrible idea, but an investor named Tom Fox encouraged him, and he was still so emotionally invested in the movie himself that he sent faxes to *60 Minutes*, *20/20*, and the New York *Daily News*. When the *Daily News* asked to interview Jawed, Nathan issued an ultimatum: Denounce the Taliban or else I'll tell the investors the kinds of things you've been saying about America and the CIA. Jawed said he didn't want to say anything "political." They must have argued for forty minutes.

And freaky things kept happening. One day six agents from the Drug Enforcement Administration appeared at Nathan's door and asked to search the files of the moving company that shared his loft. (Nathan worked there answering phones.) Another day, four police officers showed up to poke around, saying they had gotten a 911 call. At night Nathan dreamed of poisonous fogs and burning people who screamed without making a sound.

On September 30, saying he was afraid for their safety, he put his wife and daughter on a plane to Seattle.

On the morning of October 3, Jawed called to say the *Daily News* article had come out. Still hoping for the best, Nathan ran downstairs and bought a stack of copies. But there was just one line about the Taliban "holding 18 million to 20 million people hostage" and another saying that *FireDancer* "couldn't have been made anywhere else but in America" before Jawed ruined it all by saying that the Afghans were "pawns ... for the Americans."

At around six that night, Nathan met Jawed at a subway station, and out of the blue Jawed mentioned an idea for a movie about an honor killing. Then Jawed asked what Osama bin Laden would do to Nathan if he knew about the plot to kill him by posing as a journalist—and suddenly Nathan realized that al Qaeda had killed the famous Northern Alliance leader Ahmed Shah Massoud exactly the same way. Jawed must have given them the idea! So it was true—*Jawed was in league with the Taliban!*

By the time they got to Nathan's loft and Jawed pulled a contract out of his backpack, telling him that since they'd been disagreeing so much, it was time for him to take over the film, Nathan was already on the brink of losing control. He said he'd never sign, that he'd tie the movie up in court and it would never see the light of day, and Jawed retaliated with the fatal threat that pushed Nathan over the edge: "With one phone call or one letter, you will have no family!"

And Nathan did what he felt he had to do—what any good husband and father and patriot would have done if he had walked in his shoes for the last month through the dust of all those vaporized buildings and people.

Of course, Jawed Wassel's friends and relatives and defenders view this version of events as vile, repugnant, and offensive. What a preposterous story! What a pack of lies! With one voice, they insist that Jawed was a kind and peaceful man who spoke four or five languages, who loved poetry and European films, who dedicated himself to telling the story of Afghanistan through movies. He used to say that art was the best way to "thread the needle of human understanding," one friend remembered. At least three of his American friends said he was a great patriot who especially appreciated the freedom of expression that gave him a chance to tell his story. His brother, Khaled, told me that when he thought about Jawed, he remembered his brother as a man who always tried to do the right thing. The suggestion that he would bad-mouth the United States or support the Taliban is beyond insulting—it's another violation.

"If Nathan's claiming that Jawed was some sort of Taliban or terrorist," a cinematographer named Bud Gardner told me, "that's the ultimate misnomer and a complete piece of crap."

If you want to know Jawed, his friends say, look at his movie. And certainly *FireDancer* shows that Jawed's essential attitude was humane. The lead character is a solitary artist haunted by images of Russians killing his parents in Afghanistan, the woman he pursues an aspiring fashion designer who is being pushed into an arranged marriage with a thuggish Afghan man. In one scene, she cuts the face out of a burqa and gazes through the hole. In another, the artist makes a plea to stop the violence that could have come right out of a Spike Lee film.

"There was something in Jawed that made all of us believe in him," said Vida Zaher-Khadem. After Jawed's death, Vida took over the job of finishing *FireDancer*. "I should have been working on my own film, but I wanted to finish his because I believed in him. And Nathan robbed him from us—a person who would have done so much."

Backing Jawed's family and friends are the police and prosecutor and the media, who have all lined up behind the second version of this story—that Nathan was a weirdo and loser who latched on to Jawed early in the making of *FireDancer* but couldn't cut it as a producer and made people feel so uncomfortable that he slowly got squeezed out of the movie. This made him jealous and angry, and he retaliated in petty ways, such as refusing to give Vida points or credit although she had done most of his job. He was also greedy. From the beginning, one of his coproducers said, Nathan seemed to have an unrealistic sense of how much money *FireDancer* could make. So he must have seen 9/11 as a great marketing opportunity that would give him a perfect way to satisfy both his lust for money and his lust for revenge—doubly so because his contract with Jawed specified that if one of them died, the other would get complete control of the film. So Nathan began to plot his heinous crime, sending his family out of town not to protect them but to clear the way. He built a trail of "evidence" by mooning over 9/11 to his friends and ranting about the Taliban, and he cut up the body not in some kind of "fugue state" (as his attorney now claims) but in a spirit of cold calculation that shocks the soul—as evidenced by his storing Jawed's head in his freezer so he could dispose of it separately and reduce the chances of getting caught. And finally, he concocted his ridiculous tale of trauma in the most monstrous imaginable exploitation of the 9/11 attacks, literally to get away with murder. In some ways, this is the most shocking thing of all. As prosecutor Fred Klein said in various media interviews: "To use that awful tragedy to somehow justify a brutal murder is insulting." Nathan "never mentioned any trauma of the World Trade Center or the Pentagon. This was a business dispute with the victim." In another news report, Klein repeated this quite definitely: "His statement to police clearly shows the motive was money, not politics."

Nathan Powell invited this skepticism and hatred, and it's likely that there's nothing that anyone can say that will keep him from being convicted of a ghastly murder. Especially given what he did afterward.

First he went to a friend's house and watched *The West Wing*. On his way home, he stopped to buy plastic bags and paper towels. Then he cut up Jawed's body with a hacksaw and wrapped the pieces in plastic before packing them in boxes. At one point he stopped to make a phone call to a friend in California. The next day he went to work and, in the evening, put on a suit to attend a viewing of *FireDancer* at a DuArt screening room—where he came face-to-face with Jawed's brother and mother but somehow managed to act as if nothing was wrong. He even went with Jawed's brother to the police station to report him missing. Then he went home and loaded the boxes into a van and drove out to Long Island to dispose of the body, stopping at Home Depot to pick up a shovel, pick, charcoal, and lighter fluid. He stopped at the first dark spot he saw, and he went into the woods and started to dig, then stopped and went back to the van and started to drive, forgetting to turn on his headlights. A few minutes later, a police officer named Peter McGinn pulled him over.

And then Nathan started telling lies. Testifying at a preliminary hearing, McGinn said that when he approached the van, Nathan was panting "very heavily" and his "whole face, hair, neck, and shirt" were soaked with sweat. When McGinn asked his name, Nathan simply didn't respond. Asked who owned the van, he still didn't answer. Asked what he was doing, he said he was delivering a couch. Asked where he was delivering the couch, he said he didn't remember. Asked who he was delivering it to, he said a friend. Asked the friend's name, he said he didn't remember. Asked what he was doing in the woods, he said first that he stopped "to take a leak" and then, when the officer asked about the shovel and the dirt and the sweat on his face, answered, "All right, I'll level with you. I was just looking for $10,000 that I buried three years ago."

"Well, whose boxes are those?" McGinn asked.

"What boxes?"

"Those boxes."

"What boxes?"

"Those two boxes right there."

Nathan said he hadn't noticed the boxes. Maybe they were there when he rented the van. And when McGinn pointed out that he had just said that he worked for a moving company, Nathan offered to throw the boxes into the woods.

And so it continued, until at last Nathan opened the door to look for his wallet and the officer saw blood on the boxes. When he drew his gun and told Nathan to lie on the ground, Nathan started to cry. (When Nathan's lawyer took him back to this moment, McGinn couldn't hold back his contempt: "He started to cry and then he laid on the ground and he cried some more.")

There were more lies to come. While Nathan was handcuffed in the backseat of a police car, a detective named James Cereghino asked his name and address. Nathan said he lived at 317 East Seventy-third Street in Manhattan and that his roommate was a man named Ed Greissle. He repeated this again an hour later when Cereghino and a detective named John McHugh began the formal interrogation at the police station, adding that he had been living there for about a year and paid "between $1,500 and $1,800 a month." It was only after about three hours in custody that Nathan finally told them where he really lived.

By the time they got around to asking about the murder, the cops were clearly fed up. You can hear it in Cereghino's account of what happened when they discovered Jawed's head wasn't in any of the boxes. "The first question we asked him, 'Where's the head?' He stated, 'It's in the freezer at my apartment.' I asked him, 'Why didn't it go in the box?' He said that it wouldn't fit. I asked him, 'What do you mean it didn't fit?' And he just stated it wouldn't fit."

Nathan has told other lies. On the bio he released with an early *FireDancer* press kit, he claims to have been an associate producer of a Beverly D'Angelo movie called *Pterodactyl Women From Beverly Hills*. The director and producer of that movie is a man named Philippe Mora, and he told me he'd never heard of Nathan. Nathan said that he met several times with Jay Leno's wife, Mavis, and officials of an organization called the Feminist Majority Foundation about investing in the film, but a spokesman for Mavis Leno denied it and no one at the Feminist Majority remembered him either. And Kate Wood says *she's* the one who met with the Feminist Majority. "If Nathan was having three or four meetings with Mavis Leno, Jawed and I and Vida would have heard all about that."

And *lie* may be too strong a word, but it's safe to say that Nathan's memories of his skills as a producer are much different from what others remember. He tends to talk in a rather grandiose way about his "contacts" and his film experience, but Kate Wood says that she and Jawed would give him an assignment and weeks would go by and they wouldn't hear from him. Cinematographer Renato Tonelli says that Nathan was out of his league, seemingly clueless about simple things like arranging locations in advance and bringing in food for the crew. One day he got arrested for driving an equipment truck without a license, and even though it carried at least $200,000 worth of rented equipment, he just kept on driving. "Now it makes sense," Tonelli says. "There's a problem here, an underlying problem. But at that point we just chalked it up to being incompetent."

But this is where it gets complicated. Because at least part of Nathan's story is true, and he did tell the whole strange tale to police after his arrest. Technically, prosecutor Klein doesn't seem to have been lying when he said that Nathan didn't specifically mention the World Trade Center or the Pentagon. And the statement Nathan signed the next morning does narrow the dispute exclusively to business: "Our relationship had deteriorated but I had to stay around him or I wouldn't get my money." Nor is there anything in the statement about the Taliban or honor killing or 9/11. Nor did any of these details appear in the supplementary document prepared by detectives called "Oral Statements of Nathan Powell." Nor do they appear in notes Cereghino made during the interrogation.

But Nathan didn't actually write his official statement. It was prepared for his signature by Detective McHugh, and the notes McHugh made that evening show that he left a lot out: "Italian project—Afghan marries outsider. Family sends killers. Summer 2000—Afghanistan. Jawed—interview Bin Laden. WTC—increased problems. Jawed—CIA responsible. Jawed—2 faced, thought nice—Taliban supporter."

During Cereghino's testimony at the preliminary hearing, more inconvenient details surfaced. Yes, Nathan told them that Jawed was a Taliban sympathizer. Yes, he said that he and Jawed had discussed a plot to kill Osama bin Laden. Yes, he said that Jawed had "made some very unpatriotic statements." Yes, Nathan told them that Jawed had made a trip to Afghanistan just before the 9/11 attacks.

And some of it checks out. Jawed did go to Afghanistan that fateful summer. Baktash did train at a flight school in Florida. And there seems to be some truth to the Osama bin Laden story too. Several of Nathan's friends remember him talking about it at the time. So does Marc Palmer, a lawyer and building inspector who is not his friend. Reluctant to talk at first, Palmer eventually said that yes, his retired father-in-law did once work for the CIA and there was a day about a year before the murder when Nathan came over to his house to show him a trailer of *FireDancer* and told some complicated story about someone the government or the mob was after. "There were some weird machinations that he wanted me to get involved in. I don't recall much because it got very convoluted, so I sort of blanked it out."

This is the problem: Nathan faces a charge of second-degree murder, which in New York is applied in cases of deliberate intentional killing or killing with depraved indifference. To defend against this charge, Nathan's attorney—a rumpled admirer of William Kunstler's named Tom Liotti—would have to prove that Nathan acted "under the influence of extreme emotional disturbance for which there was an explanation or excuse, the reasonableness of which is to be determined from the viewpoint of a person in the defendant's situation under the circumstances as the defendant believed them to be."

This means that Nathan's case really hangs on one thing: Was he really and truly afraid of Jawed in the moment that he killed him?

Liotti argues logic: If Nathan had planned to kill Jawed, why did he do it in his loft instead of some back alley? Why did he assault him with a pool cue, a weapon of convenience, instead of a gun? Only fear explains it, and only fear explains why Nathan went through with the horror of cutting up the body because he was sure that if they knew what he had done, Jawed's family would be bound by the rules of honor killing to come after his wife and daughter.

Because no one believed his story, Nathan asked for a liedetector test and wrote up a list of hundreds of questions he wanted to be asked. In the first round, the polygraph expert asked him three questions:

1. In November 2000, did Jawed say he could set up a meeting with Osama bin Laden?
2. Did Jawed tell you that he would have supported the terrorist action publicly if it were not for the loss of life?
3. Did Jawed tell you, on 9/11, that the U.S. was getting a little of its own medicine?

Nathan answered yes to all the questions, and the polygraph expert says he was telling the truth.

But Nathan wanted to answer more questions, so his mother paid for another test. This time the most important questions were:

1. Did Jawed Wassel threaten the lives of your family that night on October 3, 2001?
2. Did you strike Jawed Wassel over the head with a pool cue in order to stop him from killing you?

Nathan answered yes to both questions. And the polygraph expert says that he did not lie.

So who is Nathan Powell, and what was going on in his mind the night he killed Jawed Wassel? Nathan's mother, Gail, is a short, plump woman with bowl-cut gray hair. She attends a Baptist church. In 1959, she was a waitress in an ice-cream parlor in New Hampshire when Ralph Powell came in and swept her off her feet, talking about folk music and socialism. After scuffling around a bit, they ended up living in Ithaca, New York, where Ralph worked at a typewriter factory and a Boy Scout summer camp before landing a job as a librarian. They called themselves husband and wife though they never did get married, and Ralph collected thousands of books and always talked about the big important book he was going to write that would explain everything.

In 1963, Nathan was born, and Ralph taught him to read and how to play chess. When Nathan was three, Ralph chased Pete Seeger up a hill so the boy could shake his hand. But later he started wanting Nathan to be perfect, which meant learning Russian and wearing a suit and tie to school and stopping all that silly talk about becoming an astronaut because that would mean working for the government.

When the couple broke up in the late 1960s, Ralph went off to live in a tent and blamed his failures on the FBI. Then one day Nathan went out to play basketball and never came back—it turned out that Ralph had left a plane ticket for Nathan at the airport.

Three years later, Ralph called Gail up and said she had to take Nathan back right away—this day, this hour, this minute.

Gail was mystified. But it's only six weeks before the end of the school year, she said. Why now?

"He's an enemy in my own house," Ralph said.

The only explanation she could get out of him was that Nathan had let ice cream melt in his dresser drawer. In a voice that scared her, Ralph made a threat: "Either you take him now or I'll put him in reform school or I'll bury him in the backyard." When he got back to Ithaca, Nathan went up and lay on his bed. "You know," he said, "my dad really wants me, but he thinks I can get a better education here."

Gail cried then and cried again telling me the story. That's the thing about Nathan, she said: Because his father was so intolerant, he always wanted to be the total opposite. He wanted to be good.

Before going to college, Nathan went all the way to Russia to check out the workers' paradise and came back to tell his father he was "totally wrong." After that they didn't speak for a long time, which is one reason Nathan was so obsessed with Osama bin Laden. "Because of my father and how I grew up," he told me, "I've always kept track of enemies of the United States."

In April of 2001, six months before the murder, Nathan's father died.

By that time, Nathan was living in an illegal loft with bedsheets for walls with his wife and their four-year-old daughter. Around that time his wife changed her name from Jenny to Maia because she wanted a new name to go with a new life, maybe somewhere out west.

The daughter of a Hawaiian blues musician, Maia's thirty and has Nathan's initial tattooed on her leg. When she talks about Nathan in the weeks leading up to the murder, she paints a picture of a man who was steadily coming unhinged. She doesn't mind that. She just wants you to understand why. She met him in Manhattan in 1996, found him too short and an "appallingly bad dresser," but loved talking to him because he was so thoughtful and idealistic. His favorite movies were *Robin Hood* and *Tombstone* and *Braveheart*, his favorite book was *The Lord of the Rings*. When he started working on *FireDancer* with Jawed, the three of them would sit on the floor at Barnes & Noble and tear the script apart. The way she remembers it, she was the first to get suspicious of Jawed, in part because she's got Hawaiian blood and Jawed took that as license to criticize America when Nathan wasn't around. "It was like my country had also been raped by America so I could understand him the way Americans couldn't," she says. She insists she isn't shading things just to defend Nathan. "He'd always talk like that. He would say Americans are just fat idiots, and if he had his way he'd live in France."

When they started to shoot *FireDancer*, Jawed would tell her every day never to trust an Afghan, that they'd been lying to one another and backstabbing one another for thousands of years. "He'd go, 'Shh shh shh,' and I'd say, 'What?' and he'd say, 'That person is Taliban' or 'That person is Northern Alliance.' " She also remembers the threats over the virginity issue and "all this honor stuff."

And yes, she heard Nathan and Jawed talking about the offer to meet Osama bin Laden. And yes, definitely, Nathan freaked out after September 11. Right away he started saying he wanted to get out of the city, that it wasn't a safe place anymore. She was there when Nathan saw the Arabs pumping their fists in victory. She remembers him getting so quiet and not sleeping, and she remembers the day he came back from that investors' meeting talking about this idiot named Eric who suggested they say something good about the Taliban. And the day he came home all upset because Jawed said something about the CIA bombing the Trade Center—and the day the DEA showed up at the loft, asking questions about Arabs, and the day she left town with a sprained ankle and Nathan wouldn't let her take a cab because he had this thing about terrorist cabbies. "It was ridiculous, it was nuts. ... It got to the point where I was crying. He'd never acted like that before."

And she also remembers Nathan saying that maybe they shouldn't release the damn movie at all. "He would say he didn't want anyone who felt like that to make money off of it, and he felt very strongly about that. And it was hard for him because he had worked a long time on the film."

When Maia came to say goodbye, she brought their daughter. Standing on a street corner in a red Supergirl T-shirt, her loopy grin shining through a mass of tangled black hair, she said, "I wrote a story for my daddy."

"What is it about?"

"It's about a wizard and a mommy and a daddy who go to the beach."

"And what did the wizard do?"

And Nathan's daughter flashes her grin, eyes narrowing with the delicious secret on the tip of her tongue:

"He turned the sand blue!"

Steve D'Ambrose is the guy Nathan called after he cut up Jawed's body. These days Steve is working on a master's degree in screenwriting at UCLA. He seems gentle and idealistic and spoke to me after some hesitation because, he said, it was the right thing to do. He said that Nathan was a good and loyal friend who loved heroic movies and stories about knights in armor, a man who dreamed of using movies to do good.

When he met Nathan in the late 1980s, Nathan was jolly, good-natured, likable. He knew a lot about Christianity and the religions of the early American tribal peoples. He's not surprised that Nathan was a failure as an on-set producer because that was never Nathan's thing. "What he always told me in film school is that he wanted to be the background guy—the invisible producer motivating the artist.

That was something I always found kind of fascinating, because most other people in film school wanted to be famous."

He also knew Jawed slightly but didn't really have much of a take on him. There was one strange incident. When Nathan and Jawed were raising financing for *FireDancer*, Jawed asked Nathan to ask Steve to go visit an uncle of Jawed's who lived in Beverly Hills. But when Steve mentioned Jawed's name, the man started screaming at him. He apologized and got back in his car and starred to drive away. "And this is where it gets really weird. He got in his Mercedes, chased me, cut me off, and then got out of his car and ran to my car yelling and screaming. I mean this guy literally chased me down."

So Steve understands why Nathan might have been freaked out by some of these Afghans. He also remembers Nathan talking about the offer to interview Osama bin Laden.

But mostly he remembers that haunting call at midnight on October 3. "It was a weird phone call, to say the least. One of the key points that stuck in my head was that Nathan apologized to me. He said, 'I'm sorry for not calling you earlier about 9/11.' Which I thought was odd, because I was in L.A. and he was in New York, and if anybody should have called it should have been me."

They talked about September 11 and the likelihood of future attacks. Nathan asked if Steve's family was okay. "And he said something else that really stuck in my head. He said that all the Afghans who were here should be put in jail."

Steve was shocked. That was not the Nathan he knew. "So I told him, 'You know, Nathan, that's wrong. That would be the equivalent of interning the Japanese Americans during World War II.' "

Nathan went silent.

Of all the people who loved Jawed, the one who spoke most openly was Kate Wood, a dignified older woman who was drawn to *FireDancer*'s idealism after a long career in educational TV. The first thing she told me was that she never felt comfortable around Nathan, even avoiding simple things like riding in a car with him. "I was scared," she told me. "There was no basis for it, but I knew that I did not want to be riding home with Nathan."

But there were good things about him, she said. She liked the way he talked about his daughter—"I would think, He's got to be okay, he's just so wrapped up in his child"—and she always believed in his love for *FireDancer*. "I heard him say to investors, 'I read this script and it made me cry.' I didn't doubt that. I still don't doubt that."

Alone among Jawed's friends, Kate was willing to say—after a certain amount of verbal squirming—that there was truth in Nathan's stories about Jawed defending the Taliban. "There were a lot of people who said the Taliban were good for some women in Afghanistan because the Russians had done such terrible things to women. The Taliban were protecting the women. I did hear him say things like that. But at the same time, he said, 'Now they've gone too far.' It was always in context."

It's also true that Jawed was secretive about going to Afghanistan in the summer of 2001, she said. Her impression was that Jawed felt that the various factions in the Afghan American community might not understand what he was doing over there. "He just thought it was better if people didn't know."

People in this story are afraid of reprisals. Maia doesn't want anyone to know where she lives. Vida Zaher-Khadem doesn't want anyone to know where she lives. It's as if the distinction between paranoia and justified fear has blurred for all of them.

During a break at Nathan's preliminary hearing, Vida approached him and hissed in a low voice. A few minutes later, Liotti described the scene to the judge: "She said to Nathan, 'We're going to kill you.' And those are her exact words."

Liotti milked the moment for all it was worth, offering to swear to the quote under oath "as an officer of the court" and demanding an investigation and extra metal detectors. The judge asked if anyone else had heard it. A court officer named Dan Robinson said he had. "Your Honor, as you left the bench she approached the rail here, leaned over, became abusive, started using foul language." But Robinson said he didn't hear the specific words.

Later, describing the moment to me, Liotti got worked up all over again. "A woman comes over and says, 'We're going to kill you.'

And after I bring it to the court's attention and the court bars her from the courthouse for the duration of the case, she doesn't say, 'I didn't mean that, didn't mean that.' To me she looked like she was very resolved and very mean and knew exactly what she was saying, and the part that's also very disturbing—I don't know who the 'we' is. I have an ongoing concern about these folks, I really do."

One night, I sat down at a Starbucks with Vida, Khaled, Jawed's friend John Roche, and Eric Rayman. Rayman, who once worked as an attorney for *The New Yorker*, had already told me he didn't want to talk about the case. "I want to see him convicted," he said. "And I don't want to do anything that might undermine that." Instead, they wanted to know what I thought of Jawed's movie. I said that while it seemed very humane, the Afghan American culture seemed depressing and crazy—the forced marriages, the obsession with virginity. Rayman immediately started lecturing me on the difficulties of "culture clash," insisting that in context, back in Afghanistan, the Afghan culture was just fine. Roche joined him, arguing that some women actually like wearing burqas. And I know that they were just worried I might not understand the cultural complexities and take away a negative impression of Afghans, but at the same time I couldn't help thinking that in the wrong circumstances, in a very dark time, if you were kind of crazed already, it might sound like they were defending the Taliban.

But the reason they met me was to talk about Jawed. He was a father figure, they said. He liked the novels of Robert Musil and the philosophy of Friedrich Nietzsche. "He used to say that through cinema we can do a lot for Afghanistan," Vida said. "Everybody thinks of us as beards and guns. Nobody knows us."

Did he fight for the Northern Alliance? Did he think the CIA bombed the World Trade Center? Did Eric say they should say something good about the Taliban? All that was off limits, and they clearly thought it despicable of me even to ask.

At one point I asked what went wrong that first week of filming.

"Nathan lied and cheated," Vida said.

"Don't talk about that," Eric said.

"Why can't we say that Nathan lied and cheated?" John asked.

Later, the incident in the courtroom came up. I asked Vida to tell me what happened. But again Eric shook his head, and she fell silent.

When I met Nathan at the Nassau County jail, he was waiting for me in a bare room with one glass wall. The fluorescent lights on his orange jumpsuit made everything seem vaguely clinical. "I have one request before we start," he said. "Please don't mention where Maia is living in your article."

Prison had improved his looks. He'd burned off his fat, shaved his goatee, cut his hair. In some of his old pictures, he looked soft and lost. He didn't look that way anymore. He answered all my questions in a quiet and somber voice, looking me right in the eye. And it was a bit odd the way he told his story almost exactly the way he told it to the cops, to the psychologists, to his lawyer. I kept wondering if that was just because he'd repeated it so many times, or if he was holding on to the narrative so tight because it was the only thing left for him to hold—or if he really was a fiendish evildoer mustering all his powers to keep his load of crap from shifting.

Two things surprised me. One was a certain sophistication; he referred to a Woody Allen movie and quoted John Lennon, mentioned that he'd volunteered for John McCain but said he believed in spiritual solutions more than political ones. The other was his anger. I expected him to be more contrite, but when he talked about Arabs celebrating 9/11 and said that "all foreign-born" Muslims should be expelled from the country, there was an icy bitterness in his voice that was almost shocking. "It bothered me that everybody was being so damn politically correct right away," he continued. "I don't know which journalist it was, Brokaw or Peter Jennings, who said they were worried about the impact on Arabs. What about the impact on us?"

Nathan's anger reminded me of the way he attacked the prosecutor in one of his written statements. "Fred Klein should be ashamed that he feels the need to conceal evidence that Jawed was anti-American. ... Fred Klein is trying to drape an American flag over an Afghan who at best sympathized with terrorists and who at worst actually aided the attackers by providing planning, expertise, information, and money. ... My life is no man's game, Mr. Klein, and you may take my life away from me, but you will never take my honor."

Before I left, I told him that I had met his child. "You have such a beautiful daughter," I said.

"Thank you," he whispered.

"It seems crazy that you would do this thing."

"Does to me, too."

In two and a half hours, he didn't once express regret that Jawed Wassel was dead.

FireDancer, the film Nathan Powell made with Jawed Wassel, became Afghanistan's first official nominee for Academy Award consideration, in the foreign-language film category. In April, in Nassau County, New York, Powell will stand trial for the murder of Wassel. In 2003, Powell pleaded guilty to manslaughter in a deal that would send him to prison for fifteen years.

THE GRIFTERS 1 AND 2

He said he had the largest penis in the world and that Jackie O paid $100,000 just to sleep with him. He said he set up a narcotics-smuggling operation so brilliant, the Mafia gave him a $20 million cut. For $500,000, he had sex with fifty women in less than ten hours, his climaxes monitored by a "scholarly professor of gynecology." Or so he told all the late-night TV hosts who clamored to have him on their shows. Soon enough, he ended up back in prison on his fourth conviction for fraud. That should have been the end of the story, but his next stop was Hollywood, a place where—as one director who worked with him said—"You know better, but you just go for the fried ice cream."

THE SONNY GIBSON CHRONICLES: TROUBLE IN MEXICO

Bill Tannen's first mistake was picking up the phone. It was some guy he didn't know, looking for a director. Usually, you refer calls like that to your agent, but a few years had slipped by since his last feature, directing Chuck Norris in *Hero and the Terror*, and a recent divorce had left him desperately broke. So he nibbled—"Sure, send over a script."

It came by messenger later that day, a written-by-the-numbers thriller called *Deadly Ice*, about a DEA agent who teams up with a

Mexican cop to avenge his dead partner. It stank, but Tannen proceeded to make his second mistake: He agreed to meet the man who wanted to produce it. A few days later he found himself sitting down to lunch with an overweight, fiftyish actor wearing what he was sure had to be a toupee—Sonny Gibson. Gibson was charming, and came flanked by two credible producers. One, Angela Schapiro, had been head of production at Scotti Brothers Pictures. The other, Reparata Mazzola, was a Writers Guild board member. But even by Hollywood standards, Gibson seemed to be inflating his claims; when he said he'd lined up a toy company to make Sonny Gibson dolls, Tannen's warning bells started clanging.

Then Gibson mentioned that Tannen's fee would be $125,000—a six-figure salary for a couple of months' work down in sunny Mexico—and Tannen felt himself weakening. At the end of the lunch, recalls Tannen, Gibson took out a silver flask filled with sambuca, topped off everyone's coffee, and stood up for a toast: "This is my director," he said. For some reason, it was hard to say no. Any lingering doubts vanished when Tannen mentioned that the script needed a little work—and Gibson handed over a wad of cash, $10,000, "just like that."

Tannen's agent at the time, Richard Shepherd, hated the deal. He took one look at Gibson and told Tannen to get his fee in escrow.

The warning bells went off again when Gibson mentioned his strange ... condition. "One day he says, 'Bill, I don't know how to tell you this,' " says Tannen, " 'but I have to wear dark pants in the movie, and you can never backlight me.' " With a hand, Gibson indicated the problem: his penis, hanging visibly down his pants all the way to his knee, seventeen inches slack and twenty-four erect, or so the legend goes.

And Gibson kept telling the most outrageous stories—all of which seemed to be hardwired to his giant penis. He said that he'd been a gigolo for the Mafia, and that Jacqueline Onassis had paid $100,000 to sleep with him. He even talked about his monstrous thing in casting sessions, scaring the hell out of the auditioning actresses, until Tannen threatened to quit if he didn't stop. (Gibson wouldn't talk to *Premiere*, however; he made an appointment for an interview last February, only to turn us away at the door. We called again in August and again he agreed, then changed his mind once more. Four days later, he filed a lawsuit against us.)

Then, late one night, Gibson called Tannen from a nearby restaurant. "He said, 'I want you to say hello to Julia Roberts,' " Tannen recalls. "A woman comes on and says she's Julia Roberts, only she has a New York accent. She says she's going to try and do the movie for Sonny, but if she can't, she wishes us all the best of luck." That, says Tannen, is when he realized "I'm dealing with a lunatic here." But by that time, he was in too deep to back out. He'd taken money, even gotten friends like Billy Dee Williams interested. So he suppressed his doubts, dismissing Gibson's quirks as the harmless eccentricities of another showbiz character—the kind of willful suspension of disbelief that happens a lot in Hollywood, where people learn early how to live on dreams and then make a habit of it. "You know better," says Shepherd, "but you just go for the fried ice cream."

Some things Tannen didn't know:

1. That Gibson had been knocking around Hollywood for more than a decade, leaving a string of disgruntled investors and lawsuits behind him.
2. That Gibson had been convicted twice for fraud and once for grand theft and specialized in the "advance fee" scam—the art of getting people to invest real money now for a big payoff later.
3. That Gibson regularly put out phony press releases congratulating himself for starring in movies that didn't exist. One, in 1991, announced that "Sonny Gibson will be getting equal billing with Tom Cruise in May 1992 for the film *Ragman*."
4. That the script for *Deadly Ice*—written by Mazzola, Gibson's longtime partner—bore a striking resemblance to a script called *Acapulco Ice*, written by one Chuck Conaway. Conaway, an ex-cop, was monitoring the situation through his lawyer.
5. That playing the fool was part of Gibson's act. As his prison record noted, Gibson's "ability to defraud and manipulate

> ostensibly 'sophisticated' businessmen is astounding. Prison counselors and officials should be cautious not to fall prey to his 'boyish charm' and folksy ways, for these are the tools of his trade."

The trouble began almost immediately. The line producer on *Deadly Ice* was the same Angela Schapiro whose presence at the get-acquainted lunch first reassured Tannen. She had read the script and told Gibson and Mazzola that she thought it could be made for about $2 million, their target price. But when she sat down and broke it down scene by scene, she found she couldn't get it below $2.8 million. Figuring they could find savings later, when they went to Mexico to scout locations and hire the rest of the crew, she went ahead and arranged for a completion bond—a crucial bit of insurance that protects investors from losing their money if a production gets into trouble. For a low-budget film like theirs, a bond wasn't always that easy to get, and Schapiro used her connections to obtain one. Instead of being pleased, Gibson and Mazzola went berserk, she says. They accused her of overstepping her authority, sabotaging the film by scaring off the investors who had committed to a $2 million film, and ordered her to shave $800,000 off the budget—without changing the script.

Schapiro refused. A budget wasn't something you just arbitrarily changed—either they had to cut the script or try to find savings in Mexico. Voicing a suspicion that they were less interested in her professional advice than in using her name to earn credibility in Hollywood, she told them she was not going to "spin a fairy tale." Mazzola fired her, refused to pay the remaining half of her advance, and sent a letter asking for the return of the $5,000 she'd been paid so far. "The idea that we would pay $10,000 for preparation of a budget which is useless to us and has caused significant problems is ludicrous," Mazzola wrote.

The whole thing was strange. It was almost like they didn't want to know what the film would really cost. Schapiro shot back a frosty reply: "I do not believe that my expertise and advice delayed the release of your funds and the start date of your project," she concluded. "I hope that it may have saved you from a fiasco."

Without Schapiro, Gibson and Mazzola failed to get a completion bond and went to Mexico without insurance.

To save the project, Tannen called an old friend named Rupert Hitzig. An experienced producer with seventeen movies on his resume, Hitzig wanted to see where the money was coming from. Gibson and Mazzola showed him documents confirming that at least $1.4 million of *Deadly Ice*'s budget was in the bank, he says, and introduced him to their investor, an elderly Glendale money manager named E.R. Whitehurst. They also showed Hitzig a contract with a Mexican company called Arena Films that promised $700,000 for distribution and even supported the claims about the Sonny Gibson dolls.

Hitzig hit it off with Mazzola, who seemed very sincere—she was a New Ager who collected crystals and had been a backup singer for Barry Manilow. She had even had a few modest hits back in the 1960s, singing with a band called Reparata and the Delrons. So when she told Hitzig that Gibson was misunderstood, that he'd been born again and was now planning to give half his money to poor kids, he believed her. Says Hitzig: "I looked in Sonny's eyes and thought, This guy's been hurt by this cruel world."

Still, like Tannen, Hitzig sensed trouble. He recalls that one day before they left for Mexico, he, Tannen, and Gibson were going over the script in Gibson's office when his secretary interrupted with a phone call. She mentioned a famous producer. Gibson picked up the phone and started talking: "Two hundred and fifty thousand dollars for second billing with Pacino? Can't you do any better?" While Gibson talked, Hitzig and Tannen watched the phone lights go out, one by one, until all the lines were dead. "And he keeps talking," says Hitzig. " 'Tell Al I'm very thrilled to be in the movie with him.' "

Hitzig and Tannen just looked at each other. What had they gotten into? On the plane down to Mexico, they considered the risks. "If we let Sonny play it his way," said Hitzig, "we might end up with the *Airplane!* of drug movies."

Tannen and Hitzig arrived in Mexico City in October 1992. Among their first hires was Claudia Becker, one of Mexico's top casting agents. But when Becker started calling leading Mexican actresses, she discovered that Gibson had already made a casting trip on his own. "They told me they had an interview with this crazy man," says Becker, "and the conversation was about what a huge potency he had, and they were shocked—they didn't know if he was serious or if he was joking."

In order to get Becker to continue working on the movie, Tannen and Hitzig had to promise to keep Gibson out of the casting sessions. At one point, Becker got a phone call from a man who said he was the head of casting at Universal Pictures, and he was looking for Sonny Gibson because he was a very good actor and Universal wanted him to play the lead in a very important movie. "It was himself trying to be the head of the Universal studio," says Becker. "I recognized his voice."

The Mexican partner, Arena Films, was also something less than Gibson claimed. "It turns out the so-called third largest distributor in Latin America had an office the size of my kitchen," says Tannen. As for the $700,000 Arena had supposedly committed for distribution, that turned out to be part of an unofficial side deal with one of Arena's two partners, a man named Ramon Cerro Cano—and when news of it reached the other partner, a woman named Gloria Mayo, she quit the company. So why were they in Mexico? "You could have done the whole show in L.A., but Sonny said he had this deal with Arena Films," says Tannen. Despite growing anxieties, nobody could quite picture Gibson as the mastermind behind an elaborate scheme. "Sonny doesn't seem smart enough to be devious," explains *Deadly Ice* cinematographer John Newby. "He seems sort of sincere, like some kid who says, 'Let's make a movie,' and it's 'Okay, Billy, let's make a movie.' "

The Mexicans dismissed him as an amiable fool. "We all used to laugh about him," says Mineko Mori, who played *Deadly Ice*'s villainess. "We thought he was this harmless man who had all this money and wanted to be an actor." Nobody had really been taken in by the press conference Cerro Cano and Gibson had held announcing that an 18 million peso "*superproduccion*" was bringing a real celeb to town—Sonny Gibson, "*hermano de Mel*." But Mazzola's presence helped ease everyone's doubts, with her seriousness about making the movie and earnest talk of spirituality, crystals, and Indian healing. "She told me Sonny was very good-hearted, he helps these children in East L.A.," says Mori.

The shoot began with all the usual high hopes. The Mexican crew was first-rate, the caterer a pro (she had once worked for John Huston), and the filmmakers had an excellent equipment package. They even had a name costar—Tannen had run into Erik Estrada at his hotel and invited him to join the cast. On October 30, Gibson and Mazzola bought the entire back page of *Daily Variety* to announce the start date of "The Mexican *Lethal Weapon*."

But once the cameras started rolling, Tannen and Hitzig knew they were in serious trouble. Gibson couldn't act, couldn't hit his marks, couldn't even talk without mumbling so badly that the cast suspected brain damage. "He is, without doubt," says Hitzig, "the single worst actor Hollywood has ever seen."

Gibson whiled away time on the set telling his tall tales, boasting that he was in *The Guinness Book of Records* for having the world's longest penis. Mori heard Gibson talk about having an orgy with Sylvester Stallone, Cher, and Madonna, and being Julia Roberts's boyfriend before she got famous.

Why did Gibson lie so much? Because it worked—Mori says that Gibson managed to seduce at least one Mexican actress she knew, promising her a part in an upcoming movie, and got another to rehearse a "love scene" over the phone. Even now, after all that happened, she can't believe it. "It's amazing how many people he can manipulate," she sighs.

Four days into shooting, Hitzig says, the money started to dry up. Gibson promised him that more cash would be coming soon. A few days later, Gibson told Tannen that all the money for the shoot wasn't really in place—he would have to fly back to L.A. at some point and get more. Hitzig was in a bind—he knew the only way the financing would ever come was if he kept shooting, and he trusted Gibson to keep his word.

Meanwhile, Gibson insisted on star treatment. Erik Estrada shared a trailer, says Mori, but Gibson had one all to himself.

After two weeks of shooting, the Mexican actors held a work stoppage, threatening to go on strike if they didn't get paid. Around the same time, Gibson told Tannen he couldn't pay him the rest of his fee—instead of putting the whole fee in escrow, Gibson had given Tannen half the money up front and promised the rest after three weeks of shooting. Would Tannen take $30,000 in a week and the rest a week later?

With his crew getting restless, Gibson promised everybody that a man would come down with the money on Saturday, Hitzig says, so Hitzig persuaded everyone to wait. Even then, nobody really doubted that the money would come. And lo and behold, that Saturday, a man arrived who introduced himself as Frank. Frank was carrying about $50,000 in blank traveler's checks stuffed into his raincoat. "I split them in $5,000 packages and everybody went to the bank," Hitzig says. "[That] kept us going another two days."

When the cast and crew saw the money, a big cheer went up. Gibson said there would be another $200,000 on Tuesday, and by Thursday they'd have $900,000.

But on Monday the Mexican actors refused to come to work unless they received the rest of their money. The crew continued, filming inserts and pickup shots.

On Tuesday, Gibson said he would go to L.A. and get the money personally. He took the 2:30 p.m. flight to Los Angeles. He called Hitzig at 2:30 in the morning and ordered him to get Mazzola on a plane to "sign some financing papers," Hitzig recalls. Hitzig refused, telling Gibson that he wasn't going to be left down there alone. He walked down the hall and woke up the associate producer, Tom Adelman, telling him he was considering shutting the company down. Realizing that he'd be held accountable for their debts if Gibson and Mazzola were both gone, Hitzig asked his cohorts to keep an eye on Mazzola. The Mexican production manager, Concepcion Taboada, stashed Mazzola's passport.

At 3:00 that same morning, Gibson called back—everything was okay, he told Hitzig. "The company would receive a transfer of $90,000 by 1:30 p.m. [that] day," says Hitzig.

Once again, Hitzig believed him. At 1:30, he was still waiting for the money. Back in Los Angeles, however, Richard Shepherd got a check for the rest of Tannen's fee. For a moment it seemed that everything would work out after all.

But the wire transfer never carne, and the check bounced. Finally, late that afternoon, Hitzig drove out to the set and assembled the cast and crew. He told them he was shutting down the film. There was no money. Panic ensued. The caterer realized she was on the hook for all the food; the transportation supervisor didn't have money for gas to get the trucks home; the PAs had run up thousands of dollars in cellular-phone bills on their own credit cards. "It was a little bit like Saigon, with the helicopters on the roof," says Hitzig.

Feeling guilty and ashamed, Hitzig said he was going to fly to California and get the money himself. (Between $200,000 and $300,000 remained unpaid.) He rushed to the airport, leaving his clothes, camera, and computer behind. The next day, as Hitzig scrambled to raise money, showing completed footage to potential investors that Gibson had lined up, things in Mexico got crazier and crazier. One of the Cuernavaca hotels told two Mexican crew members they couldn't leave the premises until the bills were paid, effectively taking them hostage. The American crew started blowing town—Adelman and production coordinator Betsy Chasse cleaned out their office and made a run for the airport.

But Mazzola was stuck—the Mexican production manager was still holding on to her passport. Gibson flew back to Mexico and arranged a meeting with all the relevant parties, and "explained" the whole debacle: Hitzig and Adelman had planned it all. *They* took the money. After all, where was Adelman? Where was Hitzig? But Sonny Gibson was right there, in that room, facing them like a man. "He made a big fuss about please, he would give us checks, but would we keep them in a security box for two months so he could raise the money?" says Becker.

The Mexicans were convinced. "Rupert never came back and his people ran away," says Taboada. At least Gibson came back, she argued. Gibson's checks were put in a security box and held by a lawyer for the actors union.

Two months later, when the Mexicans tried to cash Gibson's checks, they bounced—and the bank came after them for the check-bouncing fine. "We even had to pay that fee," Becker says.

Ronald Gene Gibson was born in Noblesville, Indiana, on June 25, 1940, the son of a tool-and-die maker. The family was comfortable, and none of Gibson's brothers or sisters ever had trouble with the law. He went to Catholic school. But Gibson had a problem with his penis. According to legal records, he was only sixteen when he got a fourteen-year-old girl pregnant. He married her and went to work as a salesman, and in short order they had four children. In his mid-twenties he divorced her and married again. Then, in 1966, he had his first run-in with the cops: As his prison record puts it, "The defendant exhibited his private parts to a girl companion while sitting in an automobile." He was convicted of indecent exposure and got six months' probation.

Gibson headed for California the same year, where he got a job working for a company involved in investigating frauds. Two years later he was arrested again. This time it was for fraud—promising people he could (for a small fee) arrange loans from a pool of money invested by movie and TV stars. Only he took the fees and never came through with the loans. He got three years' probation. While that case was in court, he turned to arranging building loans, telling his marks he was related to Jimmy Hoffa and that he had pull with the Teamsters' pension funds. Again, all his "clients" had to do was advance him a percentage of the loan as his fee—and again, he never coughed up the actual loan. To help create his persona, he traveled with bodyguards and (at some point) he dropped the name Ronald, adopting Sonny—short for Santino. Sometimes he called himself Gino Valachi.

The cops figure that Gibson got away with some $300,000 from the latter scheme. But it was his boasting that got him in trouble—appearing before a grand jury, he denied bragging about Hoffa and the Teamsters. Prosecutors showed that he was lying, and in 1971 he was convicted of perjury and got four years' probation. The following year he was convicted of mail fraud for his building scam, this time getting five years' probation.

It didn't even slow him down. Around the same time, Gibson opened an office in the Beverly Hills area, calling himself Pacific International Consultants and decorating his walls with trophies and a pair of dueling pistols. One of his first customers was the Reverend Preston Calhoun of the Cross of Christ Missionary Baptist Church, who needed $30,000 to finish building his place of worship. Sure, said Gibson—for a $750 "processing" fee. But after Calhoun paid the money, Gibson told him he needed another $400 for "appraiser's expenses." Calhoun gave Gibson another check, the appraiser came, and Gibson said the $30,000 check was in the mail. Two months later the reverend was still waiting. The next time he called, Gibson's secretary said he was in Europe. Gibson took similar amounts from the Second Benevolent Baptist Church and the Greater Gethsemane Baptist Church. When those deals went sour too, Gibson was always in Europe.

After that, Gibson moved back to bigger deals. One of his victims was a Riverside investor named James Grigsby, who says he put up $40,000 in exchange for a $2 million loan guarantee from a Panama bank which Gibson "arranged." Grigsby had to wait half a year before Gibson finally handed over the guarantee, only to discover that the bank had just been taken over by the Panamanian government and his $40,000 piece of paper "wasn't worth a fan in a thunderstorm," Grigsby says. Despite winning a 1976 civil suit calling for the return of his money, Grigsby has never been able to collect. Then Gibson met with a businessman named Robert Stone at the Riviera Country Club in Los Angeles. Flanked by two bodyguards—by this time he was heavily into Godfather mode, traveling everywhere in a long, black limousine and wearing black shirts with white ties—Gibson said he'd just finished playing golf with Dean Martin, and that he was on the board of forty-two unions and had just arranged $40 million in financing for the MGM Grand hotel in Las Vegas. Forty million happened to be exactly the sum Stone and his partner, Richard Fong, were looking to raise. No problem, Gibson said—for $15,000 earnest money.

Gibson followed his usual pattern, telling Stone and Fong five days later that he needed another $15,000. Then he said one of the unions had dropped out and he needed another $10,000. Out of cash, Stone and Fong brought in an acquaintance name John Patrick Mills, and Gibson fleeced Mills like a master, pulling him out of the meeting with great tiptoeing drama and taking him into his private office to show him—a sombrero! And under it—a cassette! It was, Gibson confided, the highly secret tape of a talk with a union official back east. He played a bit of it, and Mills heard the union guy say the loan was in the bag—all he needed was $50,000 in "good faith" money.

Mills gave Gibson $50,000 in cash.

A few months later, Mills started haunting Gibson's office, wondering what happened to the $40 million, and Gibson spun stories like a demented Scheherazade: The courier who carried the money to the union officials had mysteriously disappeared, the officials acquired the money but couldn't give it back until the new year (for tax reasons), Gibson would pay him back personally except his money was "tied up with the United States government."

Then Gibson slipped again. He'd been hanging out at golf courses in Thousand Oaks, telling people he was working on a series of instructional videos with Jack Nicklaus. But he was too flamboyant for such a small town, and the cops started keeping tabs on him—as Ventura County DA Michael Bradbury puts it, "We kept hearing about this bozo who tried to pretend he was Mafia."

One night, Gibson and a bodyguard were hanging out at their regular bar, the Los Robles Inn, when a group of golfers expressed skepticism about Gibson's Mafia credentials. "Is this the Godfather?" one of them said. Gibson flew into a rage, breaking a wine bottle on the bar and—covered by his bodyguard—slashing a computer specialist named Mike Burns on the face and shoulder. He ordered him to get down on the floor and "kiss the feet of the Mafia." Bleeding and dazed, Burns obeyed. Then Gibson ordered him to crawl out of the bar on his knees.

Gibson was arrested and charged with assault with a deadly weapon. According to Bradbury, Gibson promptly set about "trying to intimidate witnesses or buy them off." Gibson might have gotten away with it if he hadn't been so tight with a dollar—he told a henchman to show $1,000 to one of the witnesses but to hold onto the money until the case was resolved. Angry that Gibson was all promises, nothing "up front," the witness went to the police, and Bradbury's office indicted him again, this time for attempting to bribe a witness. Gibson's Riverside sucker James Grigsby also got a little revenge for his lost $40,000 by wearing a wire to help gather evidence against him.

Once more, Gibson pleaded guilty and was released on bail, only to try to bribe a city councilman, according to court documents. In court, DA Bradbury asked for a long sentence, in part to send a message to Gibson's soul mates back on Sunset Boulevard: "On any given night, the Polo Lounge of the Beverly Hills Hotel is full of them," he said. "We believe that society taking a firm attitude toward punishing Gibson will not be lost on these people." Gibson was sentenced to a term of six months to life for the assault and witness-bribery charges. A few months later he pleaded guilty to three counts of grand theft for his scams of Stone, Fong, Mills, Grigsby, and the churches, getting another six-month-to-ten-year sentence.

Gibson spent less than four years in prison, all in minimum-security institutions. Prison records show that he was a model prisoner, courteous and quiet. During his incarceration he wrote a fawning letter to then Governor Edmund Brown, saying he'd found God: "The reason that I am bringing my devotion to the holy rosary into this letter is to let you and the Adult Authority know that I am a completely different man from the man I was the day that I came to prison. I have no desire to have jet planes, limousines, bodyguards, etc., or any of the good things that make up a good front to deceive people."

After getting his parole in 1977, Gibson soon hooked up with Reparata Mazzola, who turned out to be a perfect match—just as he had dropped Ronald for Santino, she had been Lorraine Mazzola when she joined Reparata and the Delrons in the mid-1960s, and she took the name Reparata when the original Reparata retired. The original Reparata was Mazzola's childhood friend Mary Aiese, who founded the Delrons in 1962 and was the lead singer on their early hits. They grew up on the same Brooklyn block and went to Catholic school together, and Mazzola was even in Aiese's bridal party. But when Aiese recorded a hit single as Reparata in 1975—by which time Mazzola was singing backup for Barry Manilow—Mazzola fought her for control of the name. "It was my confirmation name," says Aiese today. "I did all the recording as Reparata. I felt like I had to fight on principle." The lawsuit languished when Mazzola blew town, and Aiese says she retains legal claim to the name today. But she hasn't spoken to Mazzola since. "I always feel very bad that she could do this to a friend, to put me and my family through that grief. I guess she got so caught up in show business she couldn't see the forest for the trees."

Together, Mazzola and Gibson wrote one of the more astounding books ever issued by a major New York publisher: *Mafia Kingpin: The True Story of Sonny Gibson*. It starts with a paean to Gibson's penis, blaming the growth of his criminal career on a "sleazy, fat, carny con man" who sees Gibson's (allegedly) enormous organ in the bathroom. "Eyeing Sonny's crotch, he says coolly, 'You could make yourself a couple hundred a week with that thing.' " Pretty soon, Gibson is dropping his pants in front of astonished hicks in meeting halls all across the Midwest. " 'That's just not human,' " says one farmer in the book. " 'I want my money back!' "

Later in *Kingpin*, Gibson gets a job as a Mafia hit man and goes to Sicily, where he spends nearly three years at a hit-man school right out of a James Bond movie. To teach him how to tolerate pain, for example, his Mafia teachers torture him for an entire month. They spend the first two weeks putting needles under his fingernails, the third week burning his fingers ("Sonny was able to control the pain so well, even with his burns, there was never any swelling"), and the fourth week starving him. When it's all over, they blindfold him and feed him a meal of raw birds, beetles, and worms. "Someday," his instructor tells him, "you might have to eat these kind of things to stay alive."

A few years later, Gibson is a Mafia superstar, raking in $6 million in cash every month. The financial press dubs him "the Wall Street Wonder Man." He has planes, hotels, a ski lodge, a casino in the Bahamas—but in his heart he's still a gigolo: "Every woman he makes love to leaves the island smiling. Sonny's fee for one night is $5,000. His average weekly take from this side operation is $30,000." He also—skip this if you're squeamish—has a "private stock" of very special women: "Sonny has deals with insurance company gynecologists all over the country to provide him with a list of patients who have large vaginas. The women are then offered $2,000 plus room and board to live with him."

Gibson scores triumph after triumph in the book. He sets up a narcotics-smuggling operation, and the Mafia gives him a $20 million cut. For $500,000, he has sex with fifty women in less than ten hours, his climaxes monitored by a "scholarly professor of gynecology." He rakes in another $40 million by conning some real estate developers into believing he's got a permit to build a housing development right in the middle of Great Smoky Mountains National Park. Still in his twenties, he's up to $7 million a month, and he's planning to start his own country—he has a scheme to buy a chunk of the Philippines, "build himself a fortress, surround it with a 300-man battalion of bodyguards, and live like an emperor for the rest of his life." The price tag: $500 million. He even meets Elvis, who begs Sonny to help his career: "Sonny is struck by Presley's humility. He didn't expect it from this national hero." When he agrees to lend a hand, Elvis hugs him.

Kingpin draws to a close in prison, where Gibson gets a visit from an angel. "Write your story," the angel commands. "The book will be a best seller, and the film will gross $100 million the first year."

Horribly written and blatantly ludicrous, *Mafia Kingpin* is nonetheless an amazing book, such a feverish explosion of melodramatic storytelling that it is weirdly compelling. There is even a kind of twisted con-man grandeur to it—a hardcover book! Filled with the most outlandish lies! Talk about getting over! It seems only natural that Gibson takes the angel's advice and goes back to Hollywood, this time not to con the suckers but to ... become an actor.

Gibson showed up in Hollywood around 1979, promoting himself as a hit man turned actor and pushing an inspirational motto: "Anyone can change." He approached director James Toback with a manuscript of his book, and Toback gave him a small part in a movie called *Love & Money*. The very first day, "he hit me with 500 stories about prison and the Teamsters," Toback recalls. "It was sort of like Roseanne Arnold—there was no stopping him."

And he sold his book. On December 11, 1980, he took out a full-page ad in *Daily Variety*: "International Public Relations congratulates Ex-Mafia Figure Sonny Gibson, writer-actress Reparata Mazzola on the half-million dollar sale of his life story 'Mafia and the Cross' to Grosset and Dunlap, Inc." The ad went on, predicting the movie version would "make the films *The Godfather* and *Midnight Express* look like kindergarten stories," and promising that Gibson would give away half his profits to "ghetto youth around the country."

The advance wasn't a half million dollars, and it's hard to believe that the ghetto youth ever saw a dime. But Gibson's press campaign continued—next up, a free plug in *New York* magazine's Intelligencer column: "Gibson, whose ballyhooed book is to be called *Mafia Kingpin*, told *New York* that he's including a 'transcript' of a phone chat in which the then president [Nixon] allegedly discussed pardoning a criminal in return for a bribe," the magazine said. Nixon had more serious problems on his mind and declined to comment.

In October 1981, Gibson and Mazzola took out another full-page ad in *Daily Variety* announcing "an authentic Sicilian celebration" at Laird International Studios in Culver City. Some 900 people showed up, including actor James Coburn—who had his picture taken accepting the first signed copy of *Kingpin*. That same month, Gibson landed an investor for his movie, turning over his *Kingpin* royalties to an outfit called the Sheep Ranch Mining Corporation in exchange for loans that ended up totaling $237,591.28 or so the company said in a later lawsuit.

But it wasn't until the book appeared in bookstores that the truly amazing part began: People believed it. Or at least they chose not to disbelieve it. Gibson was interviewed by Tom Snyder on the *Tomorrow* show and by Jane Pauley on the *Today* show twice. He even appeared on *Late Night With David Letterman* and talked so long—"The film that we're doing is the largest film in motion picture history," he boasted—that Letterman had to bump Jerry Seinfeld.

Print journalists were just as receptive. When Gibson and Mazzola launched a twelve-city "nationwide talent search" in November to cast *Mafia Kingpin*, Colin Campbell covered the scene for *The New York Times*: "A line of actors and would-be actors, waiting in the cold yesterday to get into B. Dalton's bookstore on Fifth Avenue, stretched around the corner of East 52nd Street like a sort of costume party. There were George Rafts and Al Pacinos, Faye Dunaways and Ida Lupinos, Steve McQueens and Ali McGraws [sic]. There were flashes of smile and snippets of costume from dozens of recent films in which hard, sordid characters rob banks and murder people but remain romantic heroes."

In the New York *Daily News*, Bruce Chadwick wrote that 1,000 actors auditioned. "The *Godfather* movies romanticized the mob, and that was wrong," Gibson told him, striking the pious note. "Actually, I think people will be eager to see my story on film, because I portray people in organized crime for the animals and killers they are."

Gibson was spending serious money. He had a cameraman videotape all the auditions, organized callbacks, printed up *Kingpin* T-shirts (on the back, ANYONE CAN CHANGE), and bought three months of billboard time on Times Square—"MAFIA KINGPIN: BESTSELLER"—for a cost that Gibson's publicity materials placed at $45,000.

Most of the journalists repeated Gibson's claims as fact. *The New York Times* printed that Laird International Studios had put up $17.9 million to make the film. *The New York Post* put the budget at $15 million and called him a former Mafia hit man. And the *Daily News* said *Mafia Kingpin* was going to be made in the spring of 1982. Grosset & Dunlap went even further on the book flap, repeating all the major lies and calling it a "true story documented by confidential records"—when there wasn't a single piece of documentation in the whole book, apart from a few vague and misleading references to newspaper articles. And what was the author up to now? "Gibson is now a successful actor who gives half his income to help underprivileged youth and ex-convicts," a copywriter at Grosset & Dunlap wrote. And Reparata Mazzola? She was "the first woman to coauthor a book and screenplay and star in the film version as well."

If journalists became skeptical, Gibson was always ready to hand out his "parole report": "Suspected of 3 hits while in custody. Known gang leader. Unstable and very dangerous. Hit man for the Sicilian Mafia. Blackmailer and highest paid gigolo for the Mafia. Received $5,000-$25,000 a night from high-society females. Records show spent 10 days with Jacquelin [sic] Onassis, many other well-known females—37 names." Identifying marks? An "oversize penis." The report was a complete fake, of course. If a reporter's doubts appeared in print, Gibson just altered the offending sentences for his press kit—when *New York* magazine wrote that Grosset & Dunlap "was leery of backing its author," Gibson's version of the story had "Grosset & Dunlap confirm backing its author."

After his talent search wrapped, Gibson appeared at schools and youth centers across the nation, warning thousands of kids against a life of crime. "God changed my life," he told schoolchildren at Atlanta's Grady High. He filed a proclamation from the California secretary of state recognizing the "Sonny Gibson Youth Foundation" and took out more ads in *Variety*. He even got Rod Steiger to agree to act in *Mafia Kingpin* and circulated a photo of Steiger posing with him in a mock scene. (All Steiger remembers now is that Gibson was "very nice," but nothing ever came of the meeting. "It was all talk.")

The truth finally caught up with Gibson, in the person of reporter William K. Knoedelseder Jr., in the *Los Angeles Times*, who thoroughly debunked his book. Knoedelseder dug up Gibson's actual criminal and prison records and compared them with the—*inflated* seems too weak a word—*insane* claims in his book. Where Gibson says he spent weeks in the prison hole, for example, reduced to a diet of mice, Knoedelseder showed there were no holes in the minimum-security prisons where he served his time. Knoedelseder's most devastating quote came from Michael Brenner, a Los Angeles deputy D.A. who helped prosecute Gibson in 1974, regarding Gibson's claim to have been a Mafia hit man: "It's like some guy telling you he was born on Venus."

Gibson and Mazzola fought back with a two-page ad in *Daily Variety*: " 'MAFIA KINGPIN' is now ready to commence principal photography. We have a top producer, top director, a distribution commitment with the major U.S. theater chains, foreign sales, and all of our locations and principal can, including, Rod Steiger. Mr. Knoedelseder can be assured that 'MAFIA KINGPIN' WILL be made and will reach millions all over the world with its universal message: 'ANYONE CAN CHANGE.' " But around the same time, the Sheep Ranch Mining Corporation filed suit for breach of contract, claiming Gibson and Mazzola had never paid back a dime of their loan. (The case seems to have not been pursued beyond the filing; contacted recently, the company's former lawyer did not recall any resolution.) Shortly afterward, Gibson filed for bankruptcy.

That should have been the end of the story. Exposed as a fraud and headed for bankruptcy, Gibson should have slunk away in disgrace. But this was Hollywood, and it was the 1980s, and Gibson's showbiz career was just beginning. Over the next ten years he and Mazzola would make hundreds of thousands of dollars—maybe millions—and even star in a real movie.

THE SONNY GIBSON CHRONICLES: HOLLYWOOD HUSTLE

Sonny Gibson came to Hollywood boasting of being an ex-Mafia hit man with a penis so long it earned a mention in *The Guinness Book of Records*. He was so colorful that everyone wanted to hear his story from David Letterman to *The New York Times*. He started raising cash to make a major motion picture out of his "autobiography," *Mafia Kingpin*, telling everyone he planned to donate half his profits to help troubled youth.

Then it all came crashing down. In 1983 the *Los Angeles Times* exposed him as a fraud. Shortly afterward, he filed for bankruptcy.

That should have been the end of the story. Instead it was just the beginning. Gibson went right back to finding investors. One of his first was a Palm Springs socialite named Rosemary Cox. Gibson impressed her by attending her church and dropping $20 in the collection plate. "The only reason I invested with him is, he said he was doing a movie about youth, and he said he was a born-again Christian, which I am," says Cox. She was also impressed with his contacts among prominent local Christians. He certainly didn't seem to need cash—he drove a Porsche, stayed at a nice hotel called the Marquis, and generally "acted like a king," she says. He showed her a thick packet of press clips, and she heard him take phone calls from some big Hollywood stars. Cox was so impressed that she gave Gibson $17,500, part of which she had borrowed. When her note eventually came due, in 1986, Gibson and his partner, Reparata Mazzola, started giving her a string of excuses—the film was about to be made, shooting was starting any day now. Cox ended up paying her loan back herself, month by month, with interest.

Gibson also worked the religious angle on Harry G. John, a fervent Catholic who put his chunk of the Miller beer fortune into charitable causes—including $52,000 to make *Mafia Kingpin.* According to an article in *The National Law Journal*, when his wife and another director of his charitable foundation sued to have him removed from his post as the foundation's head, John told the court he had given Gibson the money because he "had such an evil past and had converted."

Around the same time, Gibson and Mazzola pitched a new scheme to a Minneapolis man named Carl Pozzani. "The idea was, your principal investment would be protected by a zero coupon bond," Pozzani explains. "You provide twenty-five grand, they take fifteen of that and put it in a bond, and in five years your twenty-five is back." In other words, he would get his principal back even if the movie lost money. Pozzani gave Gibson and Mazzola $25,000, and though he did eventually get his $25,000 back when the bond matured, the $10,000 Gibson took out up front was "piddled away on something," says Pozzani, whose movie dreams went sour. And then Gibson came back, asking to borrow $5,000—this time without a bond to secure it. Again, Gibson paid Pozzani back only to return asking for $7,500. Mazzola signed a note, and Pozzani gave them the money. But this time he never saw his money again, and since then he's had the hardest time getting Gibson to return his calls. "Every time you call, you get a story," he says. "That's what they do—they borrow money and then just declare bankruptcy and start all over." He thought about suing, but what was the point?

Then there was a Houston restaurant owner named Ronnie Bermann. "He told me his life story, getting out of prison and all that sort of stuff," Bermann recalls. Convinced, he gave Gibson $200,000. But again the movie never seemed to get started. "It was continuous stalling and stalling." Finally, Bermann went to the cops and the FBI. "They weren't interested," he says. For his $200,000 he owns a share in the paperback rights to *Mafia Kingpin*—and later Gibson came back, just as he had with Pozzani, trying to raise more. He was so brazen, it was almost laughable.

Gibson went back to Cox too, and Cox was so outraged that she hired a lawyer and drove the two hours from Palm Springs to Los Angeles to make a personal complaint to the D.A. She even wrote to the California secretary of state, March Fong Eu. She says they all put her off, on the grounds that the money was too small a sum and the crime too hard to prove.

It had all been a lie, she realized, even the phone calls from the Hollywood stars. "He has buzzers in his desk so he can say, 'Just a minute, I just got another phone call,' " she says, "and then he'll supposedly talk into another phone, and you can overhear this conversation. It's really fantastic. You couldn't believe that somebody can be that crooked and get away with it."

Then, in 1987, Gibson and Mazzola actually made a movie. Months earlier, a Kansas wheat farmer named Jeff Cox (no relation to Rosemary) saw an ad they had placed in *The Wall Street Journal* soliciting investments in *Kingpin*. Cox didn't want to invest, but he had an idea for a movie of his own: *Dark Before Dawn*, about "corporate farming and how we in the United States don't realize how we're being underdogged and cheated," he says. Mazzola said she'd write the script for $25,000. "I had to pay $18,000 up front to get her here," Cox recalls. "I was pretty eager to get this done."

Cox drove down to Amarillo, Texas, to pick up Mazzola, put her and an assistant up in his own house, and took her door-to-door to do research. Mazzola collected another $7,000 and went back to

Hollywood to write the movie, adding a murder mystery to Cox's tale of hard times in the heartland. Two years later, Gibson and Mazzola found an investor, an Oklahoma millionaire named E.K. Gaylord. Gaylord paid Gibson a surprisingly high fee for an actor in his first significant role—something in the "mid-six figures," according to Barry Rosenthal, the lawyer who had negotiated Gibson's deal—and put up a "couple million" to make the movie. Gibson and Mazzola assembled a cast that included Ben Johnson and Billy Drago and hired an old *Gunsmoke* veteran named Robert Totten to direct. In a pitch letter to a potential distributor, Mazzola reportedly promised to give a piece of their profits to a foundation to help troubled farmers.

Gibson and Mazzola made sure their deal caught the eye of Hollywood—at a cost placed at $5,800, they took out a two-page, fullcolor ad in *Daily Variety* announcing the movie. The ad also caught the eye of reporter William K. Knoedelseder Jr., who then did a follow-up in the *Los Angeles Times* to his 1983 piece exposing Gibson, noting that at the time Gibson and Mazzola paid for their *Daily Variety* ad, they were being sued by their Sunset Strip landlord for nearly $25,000 in back rent.

But this wasn't just a scam, said Rosenthal. Gibson and Mazzola were "emotionally wrapped up in the film." (Rosenthal died subsequent to being interviewed for this article.) Six years had gone by, and they had not shot a frame of *Mafia Kingpin*. Now they finally had a chance to prove themselves, to write and star in a real movie to make—all the lies come true.

The plot for *Dark Before Dawn* was pure pulp: In the search for her boyfriend's killer, an intrepid reporter—played by Mazzola—stumbles across a fiendish corporate scheme to corner the grain market and drive the price of bread up to $6 a loaf. The corporation gets help from a cult of hayseeds who practice strange and bloody rituals in a barn, and Mazzola gets help from a salt-of-the-earth farmer named Jeff Parker—played by Gibson.

When it came time to shoot, Cox chartered a plane to fly Gibson and Mazzola to the area, then drove them to his farm, the film's principal location. At first they were nice, very "cordial," says Cox. Gibson was a character, for sure—"He'd come down to the gym wearing these little short shorts with his dick hanging down over his leg, got all these women talking," Cox says—but still, hopes were high.

The trouble began when they started shooting. "Sonny and Reparata wanted their way all the time," Cox says. One night, while watching dailies, Gibson put his fist through a wall. "That was kind of the turning point," Cox says. Eventually the Kansans wouldn't even refer to Gibson and Mazzola by name. They were just "the California people."

The problem was, Gibson and Mazzola were terrible actors. The evidence is still there on the videotape, released in 1989 by Vestron. Gibson is so stiff and flat that he's like a bad boy trying to act innocent in the principal's office, and Mazzola ... well, there's no nice way to put this: She looks like a cross between Patti Smith and Margaret Hamilton. There is something absurd in the spectacle of Gibson gazing at a wheat field, saying, "I get a real good feeling putting a seed in the ground and watching it grow. It goes from green to gold, you say. 'Hey, I've done something.' " The editor cut around them as much as possible.

When they saw the finished movie, Gibson and Mazzola erupted in rage, demanding that it be recut to put them back in. They raised such a fuss that, in March 1988, Gaylord paid them $200,000 to give up their rights to the picture and go away. But they continued to slag the film, even taking out ads disavowing it and threatening to take action against any theater owner who showed it. Finally, Gaylord sued to get them to desist—they had signed an agreement, after all—and they sued him right back, asking $25 million in damages, claiming that his cut of the film made them look unprofessional and "demean[ed] their acting ability." The specific charge: breach of contract and—ironically—fraud.

Gibson and Mazzola's suit against Gaylord was dismissed. Gaylord got a court order telling Gibson to stop bad-mouthing the film. In the case's eventual settlement, Gaylord's lawyer, Victor Grider, demanded that Gibson never try to contact his client again.

"I've never met anyone like him," says Grider. "He has a history of using the legal system for terrorist purposes, and he has no qualms about a frivolous lawsuit. Once he got his hooks into my client, he was like a bad cold—you couldn't get rid of him."

When the distributor of *Dark Before Dawn* finally tested the waters with a platform release in September 1988, "the reaction and reviews were horrible," Rosenthal recalled. Gibson and Mazzola went on a rampage: They sued their former landlord for $20 million, claiming the landlord had libeled them in the *Los Angeles Times* article. (The case was settled out of court.) Then they sued the *Times* too, asking for $100 million (a judge later dismissed the case as having "no merit" and presenting "no triable issue of fact"). Then they sued Rosenthal, claiming that he'd represented them in California without a license, among other charges. Rosenthal believed that Gibson had also sold shares in his lawsuit—he said that Gibson had even listed the lawsuit as an asset in a government filing. But the suit ran into trouble when Gibson's star witness froze up on the stand and admitted she was about to commit perjury. "She said openly she had never met me, it was all false," Rosenthal said. Apparently, Gibson had promised her a guitar for testifying, and then welshed. Rosenthal won the case.

"I used to say that the only person I would have trouble representing was Adolf Hitler," Rosenthal said. "I'm going to add Sonny Gibson to that list."

For Cox the experience was a total washout. His wheat field had been burned up for the climax of the film, and Gibson and Mazzola left without reimbursing him—Cox is now the proud owner of a $50,000 note on *Mafia Kingpin*. Mazzola even refused to give him a share in the writing credit, Cox says. By the end, Cox figured even Gibson's famous penis was probably just an "add-on"—"Everything else was phony," he says. A couple of years ago he got a bankruptcy notice in the mail. "My lawyer just grinned with me and said, 'Forget it, these people are Hollywood people. Just go on down the road.' "

After *Dark Before Dawn*, Gibson and Mazzola landed their biggest fish up to that point: a wealthy Beverly Hills housewife named Caryle Waldman. She had just turned fifty and looked a little like an elegant Lily Tomlin—Cartier watch, diamond earrings. Her husband had made fortunes in furniture, paper, and computers, and they took a month-long cruise every year. The Waldmans lived on Maple Drive, just around the block from Kitty and Jose Menendez.

As a diversion, Waldman and her sons had made a series of lowbudget films with titles like *Beverly Hills Vamp* and *Bad Girls From Mars*. She loved the movie business. "It was like being a kid again, at camp," she says. "You know that very intimate closeness? I was really high on it."

Waldman met Gibson and Mazzola late in 1990, in the restaurant of the Loews hotel in Santa Monica. Now the two were looking for money to make a trailer for a movie called *Maui*. The plot was a carbon copy of *Dark Before Dawn*, and again, Gibson promised to donate a chunk of his profits to the needy—this time to establish a center for abused kids. The first thing she noticed about Gibson put her off—"this terrible toupee" (actually, some sort of weave)—but Gibson and Mazzola sold hard. "They talked about all the hard work Reparata had done on the script, they were on the brink, they just needed money to complete this trailer." They promised Waldman that she would double her investment and said they would introduce her to a man named Dr. Tom Hines, who had put up seed money for *Dark Before Dawn* and doubled it. Her confidence level went up.

Once again, Gibson and Mazzola came with a legitimate producer in tow—Ron Joy, who had produced *Vietnam, Texas* for Triumph Releasing. They kept dropping the name of John Peters, former president of Francis Ford Coppola's American Zoetrope. Gibson had a professional-looking prospectus—right on the cover it read: "Prepared by: Rei Miyaucri, Vice President, Investments, Dean Witter Reynolds." It had charts showing estimated profits, and touted the investment as a "unique opportunity."

Waldman still had doubts, but she found herself weakening. "I can't tell you what it was, I did want to believe that they'd been working very hard on this," she says. "They were very urgent—I mean, the pressure was very great from them to me to listen and ... be compatible with what they were saying."

After the meeting, "the phone calls started immediately," Waldman recalls, Mazzola asking to meet for lunch, dinner, drinks—six times that first week alone. One night, Gibson called and said he had a confession to make. "He proceeded to tell me about his sordid past, because he wanted me to hear it from him rather than a stranger," she says. "It was very disarming." He warned her that people would trash him—everyone was against him. But he was really a hardworking actor and his life had changed. He was flirtatious and boyish, and though she never took him seriously, it was fun to flirt back.

Waldman's sons met Gibson and Mazzola and immediately became suspicious. They wanted to make sure that any family money loaned to the two was secured by a completion bond. But Gibson and Mazzola didn't like that idea. "It was clear they weren't interested in making the movie," says Waldman's younger son, Drew. "They just wanted the money." The older son issued an ultimatum. "He said to me, 'You cannot put family money into someone else's film,' " says Waldman. She was indignant. She couldn't understand why everyone was so vicious about her new friends. It must be true what Gibson had said—he was misunderstood. "I said, 'It's not family money but my money and your father's money, and you can't tell me what to do.' "

Waldman finally loaned Gibson and Mazzola the money they wanted—$189,000. Then her husband developed pneumonia. She put him into a hospital and then a convalescent home, and her relationship with her sons got worse. Meanwhile, Gibson and Mazzola filled the void in her life, calling every day from Maui, where they were shooting their trailer. They told Waldman they felt terrible about the family rift—"They said, 'What's wrong with your kids?' " Once, Mazzola had to call and let her know that her son's objections were getting around town, had even scared off one of the investors. Waldman was mortified.

The battle escalated. Waldman's sons tried to convince their mother that Gibson was a con man. "We talked and talked and talked until we were blue in the face," Drew says. But Waldman wouldn't listen. Finally, Waldman's husband filed for divorce, citing among other grounds his wife's investments with Gibson and Mazzola. Gibson's promotional packet about his Mafia past was filed along with the divorce papers. "It was a nightmare," says Drew. "It tore our family apart."

As the divorce dragged on, Waldman fell into a "fugue state," a kind of dazed grief. She couldn't believe what had happened to her—one minute she was Mrs. Waldman, with a house in Beverly Hills, and the next minute she was living alone without husband or sons. Now, when Gibson told his tall tales—that he was friends with Tom Cruise and Sylvester Stallone, that he had slept with Melanie Griffith and Cher, that he was in *Full Metal Jacket*, that he was Mel Gibson's brother and Mazzola was related to Governor Mario Cuomo—she didn't question them. Mazzola became her constant companion, visiting her every day. "I became very dependent on Reparata," she says. "She went to my lawyer, to my husband. Whatever letters she wrote, I signed."

That spring, Kingpin Productions declared bankruptcy. Waldman saw the notice by chance in a local newspaper and immediately broke out in a cold sweat—but Mazzola calmed her fears. It was just a formality, having nothing to do with her.

Meanwhile, Gibson needed money. He said he needed $12,000 to pay "tax stamps" or the Italian government would somehow keep him from making *Mafia Kingpin*. With her divorce in its final stages, Waldman soon had the money to give. Another time, he needed $13,200 to pay taxes on a house in Palm Springs. She wrote another check. When she learned that Mazzola had a taste for Vuitton but only had knockoffs, she bought her some originals. She even changed the beneficiaries of her $1 million life-insurance policy, cutting out her sons and writing in Gibson's and Mazzola's names. "They became my family," says Waldman. "They said, 'You can't trust your children. You can trust us.' "

The requests for money kept coming. '"It went on and on, and the deeper you go, they just need this little bit more. And I kept giving this little bit more." Waldman still has some of the canceled checks: $25,000 on March 4, 1991; $2,500 on June 4; $20,500 on December 9; $12,400 on December 18; $15,140 on December 23; $16,200 on December 26; $14,350 on December 30; $13,800 on January 3, 1992: $13,900 on January 10; $13,800 on January 13; $9,600 on January 15.

Early that year, Gibson threw Mazzola a surprise birthday party at Il Cielo. Tom Hines was there, talking about what a great investment he'd made in *Dark Before Dawn.* Gibson hired a photographer and sent a release to local newspapers. He asked Waldman to pay the bill. "He said, 'Gee, my credit card's all used up, could you put this on your card?' " That was another $2,500.

The one consolation for Waldman was Dominion Films, the company that she had set up with Mazzola. Mazzola was president, and Waldman vice-president. In late January, Dominion agreed to pay $10,000 to option a script—called *Acapulco Ice.*

That fall, Gibson interviewed a pair of applicants for an assistant position. One of them was a feisty, irreverent young woman named Chris (she does not want her last named used). After talking to them for a while, Gibson said he had to show them a bit of movie footage that figured in a lawsuit he was fighting, so they would know what they were getting into, she says. Then he added, " 'The first thing you have to know is that I have a seventeen-inch penis, and it's twenty-four inches when it's erect.' And he grabbed his leg, and all I could see was this hose that went all the way down his thigh. I said, 'Oh my God, he's deformed.' "

They went into the screening room and watched an explicit sex scene starring Gibson. Gibson used a pointer to direct their attention to what looked like the biggest penis she had ever seen. He explained that an unethical producer had pirated the footage, and they were in a legal battle. Before long he actually convinced Chris that he was "being exploited because of his abnormality," she says.

Chris didn't take the job. But Gibson kept after her, offering her $100 just to have dinner with him. He told her he was psychic, knew that they were destined to work together, and proved it by stating—accurately—the color of the panties she was wearing. One day she got a call from a man named John Miller who, in a deep, gruff voice, claimed to be a retired Warner Bros. executive producing Gibson's movie. He told Chris that he thought Gibson was "a big talent who was about to break out."

Finally, Chris agreed to work for Gibson. Like the others, she thought he was misunderstood. Then, on her first day, she walked into the office and heard, from behind a closed door, the sound of

Miller's voice. Hoping to say hello in person, she knocked on the door, then opened it—but no one was in the office except Gibson, talking in a deep, gruff voice into the phone. "I almost died," Chris says. "I wanted to turn around and walk out right then, because I knew I'd been had."

But Chris stayed and got a look at Gibson and Mazzola's operation from the inside. She saw mail come to "at least seven different aliases"—including John Miller and Jack Terry, the latter supposedly Gibson's agent at C.N.A. Management. She saw him dodge creditors while instructing her to say he was "on the set" or "in wardrobe." She suspected that he hadn't spent all of Waldman's $189,000 on the *Maui* trailer and that he had declared bankruptcy to avoid paying back the balance (the trailer actually cost about $60,000, according to producer Ron Joy). She even saw the bill for a private investigator who had found out what color panties she had been wearing, apparently by looking in her window as she got dressed in the morning. Chris, like almost everyone interviewed for this article, came to question the authenticity of Gibson's most frequent and personal boast. And, she says, she saw explicit photographic evidence. Although she couldn't see his face in it, the shape of his body and the furnishings in the background left no doubt in her mind about who it was. "I saw pictures where he was sticking it into a girl," she says. "You could see this big white plastic thing going in her, and underneath was this little teeny red thing." Says Chris in conclusion: "From his fake toupee to his fake dick, there's nothing real about the guy."

That spring, Caryle Janice—she had dropped Waldman in favor of her maiden name—was finally starting to get suspicious. She asked Mazzola where her money was, but Mazzola put her off. "She said she was the creative side," says Janice. " 'If you want to talk about money, talk to Sonny.' " But when she went to talk to Gibson, he'd always be out. "I was told he was on location, he was making commercials, he was jumping out of hot air balloons." By now, she estimates, she had spent almost $700,000.

One day, Janice says, she was standing next to Gibson in the office, and she noticed how horrible he looked. Suddenly she just woke up: "I want to know about my money and when I'm getting it back," she demanded. She told him she had an appointment with her accountant and didn't know what to tell him. "Sonny said, 'Tell him you lost it in Las Vegas.' "

On April 30, 1992, Gibson wrote her a carefully worded note: "Per your request, I wanted to take this opportunity to gratefully acknowledge payments to me in the sum of $199,000. ... I further wish to advise that in the event I receive the proceeds from 'Mafia Kingpin' for my acting services, I would very much want to repay the funds that you have given to me. ... I very much appreciate the faith you have shown in the progress of my acting career and I hope I shall not disappoint you."

But Gibson was still driving a red Porsche and living in a nice apartment, still kept his suite of offices on La Cienega. And a month later he had $1,500 to pay for another full-page *Daily Variety* ad: "Lois J. Benson Agency and C.N.A. Management congratulate our client SONNY GIBSON on his dynamic performance in the Movie-of-the-Week 'THE HUNT' "—a movie which does not appear to exist.

Mazzola followed Gibson's note up with a less friendly letter, demanding that Janice abandon any claim to Dominion Films or else she might be liable for $93,700 in various expenses the company owed—to Sonny Gibson! "We've become friends Caryle, but this matter is strictly business," she wrote.

Janice started investigating Gibson. Chris helped, and so did producer Ron Joy, who by now had also fallen out with Gibson and Mazzola. They assembled a list of other investors, and when Janice called them, she heard stories similar to her own. Janice and Joy swung into battle, calling the FBI and the police. Janice also called Los Angeles DA Ira Reiner and was advised to go to the Beverly Hills police. For a while there it seemed as if something might finally happen—an FBI agent started investigating, and Joy found a cop named Lee Jett who was looking into complaints from actresses about Gibson's audition scene. Joy told him about what happened to Caryle Janice, and Jett started investigating a case of fraud.

But none of it came to anything. The lewd-conduct case turned out to be hard to prove, says Jett, and fraud even harder: "The problem is, if we can prove he didn't make the effort to make a movie, then it's a cut-and-dried case. But if he goes and gets a cast and shooting schedule and all that, and then it gets put off and put off, then it would be really tough. It's one of those real gray areas."

Janice's lawyers told her she didn't have much of a case—after all, she'd signed all those papers Mazzola had given her, releasing Gibson and Mazzola from any claim. Finally she did file a lawsuit, and Gibson and Mazzola countersued, accusing Janice of failing to fulfill her commitment to finance their movies. They asked for $5 million in damages.

When Janice met Gibson in the deposition, he accused her of paying him $25,000 to kill her husband, and she broke down in tears. "These people are subhuman," she says. "I never knew such people existed other than in fiction. They're unbelievably evil." On the advice of her lawyer, she says, she settled the case just to stop the pain. She moved to Montana and hasn't seen her sons or ex-husband since.

Gibson and Mazzola went right back to looking for new investors, and Gibson made one of the most shameless pitches of his career to Brandon Tartikoff, the chairman of Paramount Pictures. "Dear Brandon," he wrote. "I would like to know if Paramount would consider distributing 'Mafia Kingpin' and committing to a good national release if we were to bring in $12-$15 million for production of the film." To warm Tartikoff up, Gibson dropped the name of former American Zoetrope president John Peters, just as he had with Caryle Janice, implying that Peters was working with him on the project. "I feel strongly that this film would do over $200 million for a number of reasons," he continued. "The hardcover outsold 'Godfather.' Surrounding me with an all-star cast gives the film marquee value. The unusual situation that the person who lived the life is now an experienced actor who can play the role, is a double barreled [sic] attraction. ... Because of my new career, the story has a powerful message to young people and the film audience: 'Anyone Can Change.' "

Gibson got a rejection, followed shortly by a threatening letter from a Paramount lawyer. "[You] were advised in writing that Paramount did not believe [your script] was distinctive enough from our viewpoint to justify our involvement in the project," the lawyer wrote. "Paramount has recently received a number of inquiries from third parties claiming to be in receipt of letters from Paramount expressing Paramount's interest in your project and requesting our confirmation of that interest. Obviously, if there is any such writing asserting Paramount's interest, it is not from Paramount." The lawyer wrapped up with a threat that left little doubt where his suspicions lay: "Brandon has gone out of his way to be open, courteous and responsive to you," he wrote. "It would be most unfortunate, and could have serious consequences, if his actions were repaid with improper and illegal misuse of his official Paramount correspondence." Gibson wrote back, blaming it on a producer he'd "had to terminate."

Meanwhile, Mazzola was trading letters with Chuck Conaway, the author of *Acapulco Ice*. In a letter dated July 11, 1992, she told him she was dropping the option on his script but offered at the same time to pay $7,500 if he would "relinquish all rights of any kind" to the screenplay. A few weeks later, Conaway got a peculiar phone call from Mazzola, "to the effect that she was writing her own screenplay and she didn't need me anymore," says Conaway.

Then, anonymously, someone sent Conaway a copy of Mazzola's latest script, *Deadly Ice*. Reading the script side by side is a mystifying experience—it is downright bizarre how little effort Mazzola put into changing hers from Conaway's. She turned the female British insurance investigator of *Acapulco Ice* into a male DEA agent who travels to Mexico to avenge the death of his partner—just like *Maui* and *Dark Before Dawn*. But aside from that, they were remarkably similar. In *Acapulco Ice*, for example, the bad guys cut a diamond courier's briefcase free by chopping off his hand; in *Deadly Ice*, they blow his hand off with a .357. An Inspector Cepeda makes an appearance in both scripts. It was almost as if Mazzola couldn't invent on her own—which might explain why she had formed such a tight and lasting bond with Gibson. He was all invention, while she couldn't even come up with another synonym for *diamonds* besides *ice*.

Conaway informed his lawyer, and sat back, since there was no point in suing until there was a film to sue over.

It didn't matter. By that time, Gibson and Mazzola had found a new investor, an elderly Glendale money manager named E.R. "Whitney" Whitehurst. On August 26, Mazzola sent him a letter: "With you as our [partner], not only could we make quality films with messages, the youth foundation we intend to establish with our film profits will finally be a reality."

There is no ending to this story. Once again, Gibson and Mazzola made outrageous promises, and little by little Whitehurst got in deeper and deeper. To "guarantee" Whitehurst's investment, for example, Gibson signed over the television residuals to *Dark Before Dawn*, just as he had signed over the royalties from *Mafia Kingpin* to another investor a decade earlier. "He had Whitney believing he would be getting $73,000 from one showing at one o'clock in the morning of this awful movie," says Chris. Later, Sonny even got the residuals back. "He had Whitney believing that he had to use the residuals for production money—so he had Whitney, poor, feeble Whitney, sign this thing that said he released him of any responsibility." Whitehurst ended up spending a fortune. "Whitney told me himself, 'Little girl, I've put in close to a million dollars out of my own pocket on this picture,' " says Chris.

Money from people like Whitehurst kept the gas tank filled in Gibson's Porsche and paid for more expensive ads in the trades. Gibson kept on pasting up utterly fraudulent articles under legitimate mastheads—if you believe the press clips in Gibson's publicity materials, production of *Deadly Ice* was announced in *The New York Times* and *People*. As he had before, he roped in a legitimate Hollywood PR firm to broadcast his lies—this time, Paladino & Associates. On one release, Phil Paladino's signature appeared under the claim that *Mafia Kingpin* "outsold *The Godfather*," when the truth is that *Mafia Kingpin* sold 25,000 copies and *The Godfather* sold 13 million. In an interview shortly before he died, Paladino said he wrote the release as a favor—a favor he regretted. "He keeps using my name!" Paladino said. "I never got a nickel from him!"

But as they had a decade before, Gibson's outrageous lies worked. By late 1992, he was down in Mexico shooting *Deadly Ice* with Erik Estrada costarring. When the film ran out of money after just three weeks of shooting, Gibson and Mazzola came back to Los Angeles and just kept going—they put together a ten-minute trailer, cutting in stock footage of explosions, and began trying to raise more money. They said it was to finish the movie, but since they wouldn't pay their debts to the actors, the director, or the crew, it was a mystery how they were going to get anyone to come back to work. Estrada told *The Hollywood Reporter* he would come back if they paid him the rest of his fee, just $35,000, but they didn't seem all that interested. They said they were going to hire a new director, new actors, maybe shoot the film in Italy. Over the next year the Directors Guild sued them in California Superior Court, crew member Betsy Chasse sued them in small-claims court for $1,700 (two weeks' pay), and cinematographer John Newby brought a labor board action against them for about $20,000 in unpaid fees. None of this stopped them for a moment. Chasse won a judgement for $1,700 but never got paid. Newby won too, and never got paid. The judge ordered Gibson and Mazzola to pay director Bill Tannen and AD Tom Archuleta a total of $69,775.50, plus legal costs. Gibson and Mazzola's company just declared bankruptcy again, and Tannen and Archuleta were never paid.

According to the DGA suit, Gibson and Mazzola's *Deadly Ice* production entity—optimistically named One World Enterprises—had raised $1.2 million for the movie. According to Rupert Hitzig, the movie's producer, Gibson and Mazzola spent well under a million. What happened to the extra money?

Early in 1994, I called Gibson. I wanted to ask him about the missing money, and all those plans to support ghetto youths and farmers, and exactly how many promissory notes on *Mafia Kingpin* were floating around out there. "I was just getting ready to go out," he said. "I'm doing a thing for Fox called *Decorated Hero*, a miniseries."

There was no Fox miniseries called *Decorated Hero*.

I said I was calling about *Deadly Ice*. "Come on the set," he said affably. "We're shooting during the first week of the [American Film Market], so Bill Shields can bring out top buyers." (Shields heads a distribution company called G.E.L.) I made an appointment with his secretary, but when I showed up in Gibson's office on the agreed-upon date, he said she must have forgotten to schedule it. He seemed willing to talk anyway—would I like to see his reel?—but Mazzola stopped him, apologizing graciously for my wasted drive but insisting we reschedule. After a few failed attempts on my part to do so, she called and said Gibson would only talk to me if I confined my questions to *Deadly Ice*. "If you want to know about his past," she said, "read *Mafia Kingpin*. We're tired of this rehashing of his past over and over—he's been out of prison thirteen years and people are talking about it like it was yesterday."

Mazzola mentioned that she was on the board of the Writers Guild, and instructed me to "go after the people who cheat writers, those are the real criminals." (The next time I tried to contact Mazzola and Gibson, Gibson sent a fax agreeing to my request to do an interview for "a nice story." I faxed him back saying I never promised a nice story. Four days later, Gibson filed a suit against *Premiere* and me.)

Next I called Whitehurst and told him I wanted to ask about Gibson. He sounded like a nice old man, very polite. "You should get ahold of Bill Shields," he said.

Shields didn't have much to say. He saw the footage from Mexico, liked it, and contracted to handle international distribution on the film when it was done. Outside of that, he didn't know much. "I know he's still working on getting it finished," he said.

Didn't Shields check Gibson out before lending Gibson his good name? "I had no reason to check him out," Shields said, getting a little testy. "He came with the footage, he's been around in the business."

So why did Whitehurst have the impression that Shields was some kind of representative for the film? Shields said he had no idea.

Next I called John Peters, who said he was "not a participant" in any production of Gibson's. "I am acquainted with him," he said, speaking stiffly. So why was his name on Gibson's prospectus? "I don't think I'm acquainted with that fact," he answered. After two more questions, Peters stopped me. "I don't wish to continue this conversation," he said. I said I'd fax him the prospectus using his name, so he could comment. He agreed, but he did not respond to the fax or return a subsequent call.

I called Rei Miyauchi, the Dean Witter analyst who had worked on the prospectus. Miyauchi said he had written it as a personal favor to Gibson, a tennis partner, and when he found out Gibson was using the Dean Witter name, he immediately asked him to stop.

I also called the Writers Guild. Had they ever gotten complaints about Mazzola? What qualified her to be a board member? Writers Guild spokeswoman Cheryl Rhoden said they had no record of any complaints. Mazzola campaigned for office and was elected in 1992, and was voted out in her next election, in '94.

I also called Tom Hines. Had he really doubled his money with *Dark Before Dawn*? Hines would not return my calls.

Through 1994, the DGA pursued Gibson in bankruptcy court. At one hearing the bankruptcy trustee asked Mazzola what assets One World had. There were no assets, Mazzola said. What about the negative of *Deadly Ice*? That was complicated—there was some confusion as to the copyright status. Where was that negative? One of the actors had seized it, and Mazzola didn't know where it was.

And who was that actor?

Sonny Gibson.

Mazzola brought along a letter from Gibson saying he had the negative stored in a safe place in Italy, and he was going to keep it because he was out for more than $1 million. There was no documentation of Gibson's investment.

In April 1994, Mazzola and Whitehurst appeared together at another bankruptcy hearing. Whitehurst had turned up on the One World papers as a 50 percent owner of the company, and by extension a 50 percent owner of the company's debt. On the other side were various creditors, including *Deadly Ice* crew members, the DGA lawyer, and a lawyer for Gibson's travel agency. In a humble and straightforward manner, Mazzola said that Gibson had never been a partner of One World, but he had paid to make the movie, so she didn't think he'd really stolen the negative. It was his.

Where were the *Deadly Ice* accounting books, the DGA attorney wanted to know. "Down in Mexico," said Mazzola.

If Gibson wasn't a partner in One World, why had he signed this One World document, the lawyer asked, brandishing a piece of paper.

"I don't know why," said Mazzola.

"I would like to repeat that you are under oath," the bankruptcy trustee, Gilbert Vasquez, told Mazzola.

"I don't know why he signed it," Mazzola repeated.

The DGA lawyer whipped out another document. If Gibson wasn't part of One World, why did this document say he owned 25 percent of the company? Mazzola looked it over. "I didn't type this," she said.

When it was all over, Vasquez said he was going to subpoena Gibson and get to the bottom of the matter. Mazzola gave him an earnest smile. "I hope I did all right," she said. "It's a complicated business, and I'm not that sophisticated myself."

Out in the hall afterward, the creditors didn't have much hope. They were pursuing the bankruptcy case simply because it was the only thing they could do. None of them expected to see a dime.

And yet, after everything, Newby was still something of a believer. "The weird thing is, Reparata wants to make a good movie," he said. "She really cares about the script and making it work. Then you put Sonny in there, and it all just falls apart."

By that time, Mazzola and Gibson had started a new company called Magik Mountain Pictures, according to the DGA. All they needed now was an investor who believed in magic. But that was no problem. Right here in Hollywood—and everywhere people dream Hollywood dreams, from the wheat fields of Kansas to the restaurant districts of Houston—there is one born every minute.

THE GUN KING

David Lewisbey was a high school football star from the suburbs of Chicago, who graduated with straight As and a scholarship to the University of Houston. When he came home for Christmas break, he was arrested for smuggling hundreds of guns across the state border in a rented van and selling them on Facebook to members of the Gangster Disciples street gang. The judge who sentenced him to the longest term possible under the law—seventeen years, just three years short of the average sentence for first-degree murder—said he deserved it because he put guns "into the hands of gangbangers."

The Gangster Disciple opens his phone and thumbs through some of the pictures on his message app: Glocks, Smith & Wessons, an AK-47, all arranged neatly on coffee tables and in dining rooms, five in one shot, seven in another, fifteen in another. There's even an old cowboy revolver with a wooden handle. "This is just from the last week," he says. He's been saving them up for me.

"What is that?" I ask him. "A Colt?"

"Something like that," he answers.

I point at a black tactical weapon, the kind soldiers and SWAT teams carry. "What's that?"

"An M4."

"And these are all being offered to you?"

He nods. "Mmm-hmm."

The Gangster Disciples are Chicago's largest and most notorious gang. They live in the heart of Chicago's murder zone, the five troubled neighborhoods in South and West Chicago that generate nearly 40 percent of the city's murders and surrender their residents to prison at rates as much as forty times those of the city's most crime-ridden white community. The Disciple sitting next to me—I'm going to call him TJ—is a good-looking guy in his late twenties, dressed in jeans and a Billionaire Boys Club T-shirt, a black acrylic watch cap, and a brown flight jacket with an American flag on the shoulder. His belt has a big gold M for a buckle and cost a lot of M too: $500 retail.

He was born and raised in a neighborhood called the Wild 100s, the hottest hot spot in the murder zone, and joined the Gangster Disciples when he was ten or eleven years old. He lost a few feet of his intestines after getting shot on the street. And he lost a few years in prison.

I met TJ because I was looking into the case of David Lewisbey, a middle-class college kid who was arrested in 2012 for trafficking guns from Indiana to Chicago and became a human symbol of gun violence, invoked by everyone from the *Chicago Tribune* to Fox News to President Obama. At his sentencing, the judge called him a perfect example of how guns "get onto the streets of the city of Chicago, into the hands of gangbangers who then shoot them and kill people with them." He gave Lewisbey the highest punishment possible under the law—seventeen years, just three years short of the average sentence for first-degree murder. It was the longest gun-trafficking sentence anyone at the court could remember.

But looking at crime through the eyes of the authorities is like diagnosing an illness by asking the doctor how he feels. You might learn enough to treat the obvious symptoms, but you'll never understand the underlying disease. How did a college boy like Lewisbey get mixed up with a street gang? Was it just mutual greed? A sense of shared danger? Did he come to embrace their vision of the world? Could that explain why guns became as synonymous to Chicago as deep-dish pizza?

So I tracked down TJ. Two minutes into our first phone call, he said he knew the case well. He'd followed it from arrest to trial and even knew some of the people involved. "They really railroaded him," he said. "The sentence for selling guns is zero to ten. No way you're going to get the max unless you have multiple felonies."

But why should he talk about it? What was in it for him?

Because Lewisbey's story points to the larger mystery, I said. Why does America have such astoundingly high tolerance for gun violence? Why does it have so much violence?

Gun-control advocates tend to blame high rates of gun violence on high numbers of guns, which is understandable because the two rates line up like identical twins. Second Amendment fans put the blame on modern culture. As Indiana state Senator Jim Tomes put it during one of the many battles between Indiana and Illinois over Indiana's permissive gun laws, "It doesn't matter where the guns come from. It's a societal problem in Chicago."

This makes Chicago the perfect entry point to a deeper understanding of America's endless plague of gun violence.

Although it isn't actually the most violent American city, a distinction traded between smaller cities like St. Louis and Detroit, it's much more violent than any other large American city—in the year Lewisbey was arrested, its murder rate was nearly three times that of New York. But easy access to guns hasn't caused the same problems in New York and Los Angeles, as the NRA frequently points out: that same year, Chicago police confiscated nearly nine times as many guns as the police in New York City.

Supply is always dependent on demand.

From there, a long series of questions flowed. Chicago's gun culture had become so normalized that even an ambitious young man from a middle-class Chicago family could see a little arms trafficking as a plausible side job. How did that happen? Why is the demand side so high? What is different about Chicago? Could looking at such an extreme case help us understand the patterns of that kind of change? Could it teach us how to intervene before the demand for guns starts feeding on itself?

"If you came to Chicago," TJ said, "I could blow your mind."

I already had a ticket, I told him. But he veered off into other topics, meandering from one to the other while probing my attitudes on race, politics, and the criminal justice system. He challenged me with outrageous contrarian statements. "Once again, you're buying the media narrative. There's no spike in crime. They're not cracking down on guns. This shit happens every day."

When he was satisfied with my answers, he said he'd take me around. Not because it would do any good, but just to get it off his chest. "I want to show you certain things and certain places to prove a point," he said.

"What's the point?" I asked.

"I want to show you the trap we're in."

At Fort Dix Federal Prison, David Lewisbey is already waiting at one of the laminated tables in the visiting area. He's wearing prison khaki, his hair is in dreadlocks, and he's down to 250 pounds—he got ahold of his nutrition, he says.

He's calm and very serious. His friends told me he was a fun-loving people person, "always a happy dude," but today there's no small talk. He's been in prison six years, with another eleven to go, and he's ready to vent.

Item one: a magazine article. He takes the stapled pages out of a manila folder and pushes them across the table. The story's about a raid on one of El Chapo's hideouts, and the opening spread is a police-evidence photo of seven guns on a stack of $100 bills bigger than a king-size bed, $207 million in all. It's identical to a photo the prosecutors used against him, he tells me. "They said this was the profit and weapons from my purchases. I said, 'Judge, this isn't mine.' " He even remembers the file number: Exhibit 41D. In dreams and idle moments, it comes rapping and tapping at his chamber door: Exhibit 41D, nevermore. It's one of his symbols of the world's injustice.

He's not saying he didn't buy and sell guns. He did, and lots of them. He went to those Indiana gun shows and scooped up everything that appealed to him. Some he kept; some he sold to friends. But thousands of other Americans did the same thing. He was just the unlucky guy who got picked to be the scapegoat for gun violence, someone they could punish in public before going back to doing the same thing they were doing before. "From the president to the governor to the mayor of Chicago," he says, "I was used for political gain."

The day it all started, he was just back from the University of Houston for the Christmas holidays and vigorously celebrating his twenty-third birthday, sleeping late and leaving his clothes on the floor. He hit the garage-door opener and slipped out past his mother's Mercedes. He was on his way to a party.

He got five miles. The fleet of police cars came out of nowhere, lights flashing. He stopped in the middle of the highway, and ATF agents came bursting out of their doors. Next thing he knew, he was in the back seat of a squad car, and an ATF agent was asking if he knew someone named Winston Geralds, also known as Worm.

"I don't know the guy," he said.

We have information that proves different, the ATF agent told him.

"Okay," Lewisbey said, "we know each other."

The agent told him they had enough evidence to put him away for a long time, but they might be able to get him a break on his sentence if he agreed to make recorded calls to his customers. That's when Lewisbey made the snap decision that turned the course of his life.

"You've got me," he said, "but I ain't doing nobody else."

His timing couldn't have been worse. Ever since the Columbine High School killers slaughtered their classmates with guns bought from unlicensed gun-show dealers, Democrats across the country have been at war against the "gun-show loophole," a laxness in the law that lets people sell weapons from "personal collections" without doing background checks or keeping sales records. Because twenty-one states permit the loophole and twenty-nine states don't, the smuggling market has become so tempting that estimates of the number of criminally involved guns sold as "personal" weapons at gun shows range from 23 to 33 percent. Police officials in Chicago say that out-of-state guns account for nearly 60 percent of the guns found at crime scenes. Now the media was back to calling the city the Murder Capital of America, and the new Democrat in office was firing off one gun-control proposal after another—a stricter registration program, a ban on concealed handguns, another on assault weapons, another on high-capacity magazines. But the mayor's biggest target was the unregulated sales at gun shows just across the state line in Indiana, the source of 20 percent of the guns Chicago police officers seize at crime scenes. On the steps of city hall, Mayor Rahm Emanuel told reporters that "transfers of illegal guns" should concern everyone, "whether you are a Democrat, whether you are a Republican, whether you're rural or urban or suburban, whether you're from Illinois or Gary, Indiana."

Lewisbey had the curse of a colorful story too. A twenty-three-year-old high school football star with straight As and a football scholarship, he was accused of buying his wares with a big wad of cash, stuffing them in a duffel bag, driving them across the border in a rented blue van, and selling them to the Gangster Disciples. One of the guns had been used in a double shooting just a few weeks later. Also, Lewisbey weighed 300 pounds, and his nickname was "Big Man."

The media ate it up. While he was still trying to make bail, the *Chicago Tribune* called his case "a textbook example of how criminals can exploit existing gun laws." During his trial, WGN-TV said Indiana's gun-show loophole was "why this case against Lewisbey and his partners is so important." CBS featured his "gun-smuggling scheme" in a segment called "Chicago Reels From Another Week of Violence." Obama referenced him during another battle to close the loophole. "Folks will go to a gun show and purchase a whole bunch of firearms," the president said, "put them in a van," and deliver them to the streets of South Chicago. Lewisbey's prosecutors responded to the public mood, charging him with one count of unlawful sale of firearms, two counts of unlawful transportation of firearms, and two counts of crossing state lines with the intent to "engage in the business" of selling firearms without a federal license.

Lewisbey sighs in frustration. "They made me sound like the Chapo of Chicago," he says.

He thinks he has a shot at a new trial because of United States v. Hubbard, a precedent he dug up in the prison law library, but he has to represent himself because he's broke, and his mom already spent at least $60,000 on useless lawyers.

"I'm so tired of this," he says.

We take TJ's car because it has tinted windows. As he pulls out of the hotel parking lot, a black Ford Explorer slips in behind us. He stomps on the gas, blasting forward half a mile before the Explorer gets through the light. He zooms up an on-ramp for South Chicago and slaloms through gaps in the traffic for a mile or two to show off his skills, then slows to ordinary reckless speeding.

A few minutes later, ten at most, one of his phones rings—he has one in his lap, one in a cup holder, and a couple of others stashed away somewhere—and he tells me to turn off my audio recorder. A moment later a raspy male voice comes through the dashboard speaker. A guy he knows has fourteen or fifteen guns available, the man says. The guy even has "a ten," a 10 mm handgun known for its big bullets and destructive power—and a kick that proved too strong for FBI agents, who stopped using it in 1988. "Who makes the ten?" he asks.

TJ usually sounds remote or grumpy, but he's never in a hurry. "Glock makes one," he says. "Smith & Wesson makes one."

"I want that motherfucker," the man says. "I told him, 'I'm ready right now.' "

Problem is, they're waiting on somebody they call Dude. It isn't clear whether Dude is financing the purchase or part of the purchase or if he's their gang leader, but nothing can proceed without him. They'll just keep in touch and stay ready.

A few minutes later, TJ takes an exit ramp into the Far South Side. He drives a few miles and turns into a shabby residential neighborhood, stopping in front of a narrow two-story house. Standing vacant and alone in a weedy lot, it's a row house without a row. He leads the way up the cracked cement sidewalk to a metal gate. "This is one of our buildings," he says in a confidential voice.

Inside, it's a construction site. TJ just tiled the kitchen and bathroom, and now he's redoing the floors—the floorboards currently stacked in the corner will go along the walls, stained lighter to brighten the room. The building cost less than fifty grand, and they expect to get $1,500 in rent, so it's a nice little investment.

He goes upstairs and comes back with a big bag of weed. Plopping it down on the kitchen counter, he digs out a scale and starts weighing it out three grams at a time. This is just a sideline, he says. He's got all kinds of deals going. He's vague about the details, but he drops a couple of references to "swipes," which is slang for credit card fraud, and mentions an interest in computer scams. He doesn't run bitches, he says, but he doesn't judge the ones who do. Down here you have to hustle 24-7. Hustling is a way of life. Everybody's on a cliff face, reaching for a rope. That's what people from outside don't get. They have opportunities. In South Chicago, all people have is obstacles. "We're two different worlds," he says, "and neither one understands the other, but the world with all the power doesn't give a fuck about the world beneath it—it never has and it never will. I live in reality; I don't live in a dream world. One plus one equals two, no other way around it."

Weaving in and out of the side streets, TJ pulls up to a small dark house and leaves me in the car, engine running. A few minutes later, he comes out of the house and slips the car into gear. He stops at another house and then another. This leads us to the Wild 100s, where he slows down.

The neighborhood doesn't seem so bad at first, just row after row of two-story saltbox homes with little yards, some with porches and porticos. As we pass a house with Christmas lights in the windows, he says, "That's where I grew up." But after a few minutes the dark shadows between the buildings get darker. Some of the houses have bars on the windows. Some of the streetlights are broken.

TJ knew the rules by middle school. This side of the block is Gangster Disciples—the other side is the Vice Lords. If you met a girl at the mall who lived three blocks in the wrong direction, there was only one good move: "Bitch, you gotta come meet me on the corner, but I'm not stopping. You gonna be right there, or I'm gonna be gone." He joined the Disciples when he was ten or eleven. It was fun at first, mostly just hanging out with the guys and smoking weed.

The downside risk was a big persuader too. "If you say no, motherfucker knows where you live."

We drive on, and he points to a bare stretch of sidewalk. "That's where I got shot," he says. It was a gang thing, a business dispute.

I ask him how often conflicts like that come up. Once a year?

"Fuck, nah. I wish."

More than once a year?

"Maybe about six," he says. "And that's just me personally."

"Even after you got shot?"

"Of course," he says. Getting shot isn't a get-out-of-gang card. When the call comes, you gotta show up. The streets are like prison that way, ruled by a law outside the law. Which is another damn good reason to buy a gun. "With a gun you can get a dude in a choke hold and put the gun to his fucking head and say, 'You ain't gonna fuck with me no more. Right?' " TJ says. And not because you're a thug with no father—because it's the best move on the table. "You gotta apply pressure. You don't apply pressure, motherfucker gon' think you a punk, so now he gonna try you."

TJ takes pride in his criminal skills. He always parks back end in for a fast getaway, never misses a turn on the back roads, never hurries a decision, and rarely drops his guard. He builds an impression of power by dropping hints of big scores and a careful investment strategy. Walking out of a restaurant one day, he noticed another car parked back end in and veered off at a 90-degree angle—an evasive maneuver, almost a reflex. As I walked on, blithely unaware of any conceivable risk, he turned back to me and hissed: "You're thinking of the wrong things!" Which meant that he was thinking of the right things, that he was closer to reality and the laws of survival. Like a medieval knight practicing his jousting or a missile crew caught in the drama of a countdown, he had learned to take pleasure in the proximity of death.

Now his phone's vibrating again. He puts it on speaker, and another low male voice comes out of the static: Something something Ruger.

"It's definitely going to blow your ass down," TJ answers. "I'm going to come check it out."

"I'll show you on FaceTime," the other man says, and a moment later the screen of TJ's phone shows a table covered in guns. The camera zooms in on a big handgun.

"That motherfucker's chunky," TJ says. "What's it hold?"

"Eighteen."

"Let me get that," TJ says.

When he breaks the connection, he tells me he's not buying all these guns to sell. Sure, he takes a little cut for his trouble. But if you get a great deal on a hundred rolls of toilet paper and take a little cut when you pass them on, does that make you a grocery store? The point is, he gives most of the guns he buys to his friends. Because then his friends will be safe, and when his friends are safe, he's safe.

Between 2007 and 2017, Chicago police didn't make a single arrest for gun trafficking. That's because there's no federal law against gun trafficking, and all violations of the existing laws are so difficult to prove: It's illegal to "engage in the business" of selling guns without a license, but the statute doesn't say how many guns you have to sell to engage in business, and people in states like Indiana can still buy or sell as many guns as they want without a license for "improving or liquidating a personal firearms collection." It's illegal to sell a gun to someone from another state, but it's hard to prove that someone did it unless you catch him in the act. It's illegal to knowingly sell a gun to someone who plans to use it in the commission of a crime, but it's hard to prove the "knowingly" part unless you capture the trafficker's inner thoughts in writing or audio. It's illegal to lie on the application to purchase a legal gun, which gives prosecutors a small but crucial opening against "straw purchasers" who are secretly buying a gun for someone else. Except you don't have to fill out an application when you buy a gun from an unlicensed dealer at a gun show.

Because of this legal minefield and all the loopholes, prosecutors in Chicago usually charge traffickers with "unlawful sale of a firearm." But the maximum sentence is only five years, which makes the expense and time investment of a court trial a huge lift for a small win.

These obstacles posed a daunting challenge for Chris Parente, the lead prosecutor in Lewisbey's case. But a win on gun trafficking in the middle of the new mayor's crackdown on guns would be a political success of significant proportions, and the evidence his team assembled against Lewisbey seemed overwhelming: They had video of Gangster Disciples selling the guns Lewisbey bought in Indiana to a confidential informant in five deals over the course of a single weekend in April 2012. They had testimony from the gun-show dealer who sold him the guns and the Gangster Disciples who sold them, even a witness who would testify that he saw Lewisbey lurking in an alley, gun in hand, while his gangster go-betweens made one of the deals with the confidential informant in the street. Prosecutors also had dozens of incriminating texts from Lewisbey's phone and social media accounts—"Cuzzo, you don't know nobody that need some bangas" was one of the milder ones. And if all that weren't enough to prove he was "engaged in the business," Parente had the startlingly blatant status updates on his Facebook page, BigDaveAgainstTheWorld:

You don't want to live my life. It's dangerous. I must keep a banger.

I would put some real shit on here but I ain't trying to get indicted. Feel me?

The loudest one in the group be the first one the feds come get.

Lewisbey's phones and Facebook accounts provided a rich trove of incriminating evidence, including 113 celebratory photos of guns and cash he took and often posted on a public page for the whole world to see—an Intratec firearm, a Glock, a silver revolver, a Ruger in a form-fitting gun box, two rifles, three handguns, a stack of cash, cash and a Glock, stacks of cash on a car seat, a Glock on a man's lap, a stack of cash and a SIG Sauer handgun.

A number of photos were recovered from David Lewisbey's cell phone, including photos of thousands of dollars in cash, one of him holding cash, a bundle of bills, a Glock handgun, a type Lewisbey sold, an FN pistol, and a SIG Sauer handgun, a type of gun Lewisbey was known to have bought.

According to the United States District Court, Northern District of Illinois, Eastern Division:

On March 31, 2012, three weeks before the gun deals, he snapped a picture of cash in a McDonald's bag.

On April 22, twenty-six minutes after the first deal, he took a shot of cash stuffed into a glove compartment.

Thirty-nine minutes after the deal, he shot another pile of cash, and this time the serial number of the $100 bill on top matched the serial number of one of the bills the ATF's confidential informant used to buy Lewisbey's guns.

To prove that Lewisbey also tried to obstruct justice, the prosecutors had a formidable piece of evidence in the phone calls Lewisbey made to his mother from jail: "If you talk to Worm, tell him to go ahead and get put up," he told her. "As long as he stay where he at and stay away from me for a minute, I'm cool." An ATF slang expert was prepared to testify that "get put up" means "go hide." Why would Lewisbey tell a member of his crew to hide if he weren't guilty?

To TJ, the prosecution had it wrong, wrong, wrong. On the street, Lewisbey had a reputation for being a warm guy with a large group of friends—from the underworld to sports to college. Anything you wanted to know about, from scholarships to business to fraud and drugs, he knew somebody that could help out. But guns and drugs weren't his hustle. "Don't get me wrong—he probably dipped and dabbed here and there," TJ says. "But as far as the street perspective of it, I know for a fact that he wasn't living that life."

Up ahead, on another dark block of saltbox houses, a big man sits in a car under a driveway light. TJ slows the car down to say hello. "You stopped calling me," the man says.

"I ain't your bitch," TJ answers. "I ain't finna blow your line down."

The teasing goes on for another five minutes. When they're finally warmed up, the man hops in the back seat, and TJ parks by an empty lot at the end of the block. The subject is guns.

"In Chicago," his friend says, "motherfuckers want a gun before a car. I don't give a fuck how old you is, you got some money, you get you a gun."

I asked him why.

"Your gun, that's your police," he says. "I have a problem, I'ma call my gun instead of call the police."

Beefs move fast and cops move slow, TJ says, at least in their neighborhoods—in wealthier areas the response time is much faster. So here the do-it-yourself ethos reigns. "My guy call me, tell me they killed his cousin? Ain't no talking, ain't no calling around," TJ says. "We gon' go over here, grab the shit, load up, wipe them motherfuckers down, get the cars, do what we gotta do."

As brutal as this may sound, crime researchers and legal analysts say that "legal cynicism" and do-it-yourself justice are natural responses to a state that fails to maintain civic peace. The inevitable outcome is revenge cycles, factional war, widespread traumatic stress, and the perverse urge to repeat the traumatic event—black men, mostly young black men, commit 71 percent of Chicago's murders, and more than half of the city's murder victims are also young black men, a staggering number considering they're only 4 percent of the population. Just running with the wrong crowd raises their chances of being killed by 900 percent. The death rate of young men growing up in those five embattled neighborhoods is twice as high as the death rate of soldiers in Afghanistan. And the cycle of trauma and revenge replicates itself, spreading through the murder zone like an infectious disease.

"Have any of your friends been killed?" I ask.

"Hell, yeah," TJ's friend says. "Every year somebody get killed, feel me? All the way to mistaken identity and shit."

And how many of their friends have guns?

"Everybody," TJ says.

"Everybody," his friend repeats. "Everybody I know got a gun."

And how many guns do they own?

"About thirteen" TJ says. "I got three or four rifles and ten handguns."

"Shit, I can't even tell you," his friend says. "I lost three this year, motherfuckers stealing them. Guns is in high demand. And guns are money too—you can sell one or use it to rob a motherfucker. You got a gun, you poppin'."

They know about America's long fight to keep guns out of black hands, from the "black codes" passed after the Civil War to Ronald Reagan's embrace of gun control right after the Black Panthers held an armed protest, and their conclusion is the same as all red-blooded American gun owners. "It's how you use them, for dumb reasons or good reasons," TJ's friend says. TJ upgrades that with a militant defiance straight out of the NRA playbook: "That's my constitutional right, the right to bear arms! You mean to tell me because I have a drug felony or a gun felony, you're taking my constitutional right? Well, fuck that!"

But why isn't one gun enough? Or three? Or five? Why do they need so many? Doesn't that just multiply their chances of getting shot?

"Cops get incentives when they get a gun," TJ says. "They get a $1,000 bonus and a week off."

The "incentives" are an urban legend, Chicago police say, but the hunt for guns is certainly fierce: Chicago police seized guns at a rate of 277 for every 100,000 citizens, more than three times the total of Los Angeles and New York combined. From the perspective of the street, TJ and his friend say, this was because the cops had become so thirsty. You'd be driving along perfectly sober with your license and registration, and the cops would just say, "Fuck probable cause—get outta the car." If they found weed, they'd hit you with "Give me a gun." Rat somebody out to cover your bare ass, in other words. Which meant you couldn't carry a gun when everyone on the street had so much rat-suspicion and rat-paranoia up their own asses, they were ready to lash out at any stranger that walked by—especially when the stranger looked like them. If the stranger embraced the same defiance, the same hunger for manhood in a hostile world, he was the perfect depository for their rage, a sensitive instrument calibrated to register every contour of their grievance. Which meant you could get your ass shot off at any moment.

The result was a classic example of unintended consequences. Because the police were so thirsty for guns, guys in the hood had to stop carrying. But hood rats couldn't tolerate the risk of being left out in no-man's-land without protection, so they were smuggling and selling and buying more guns than ever. If the cops took one gun, they replaced it with two. They were stashing Glocks in secret cubbyholes and abandoned lots all over the city.

"My banger's not on me, but it's not far," TJ says.

"You need a gun everywhere," his friend says.

With the best of intentions, the police created the market incentive for an arms race.

But now they're distracted. "We gon' see one in a minute," TJ's friend says.

They're both squinting through the back window, looking for movement.

"I was just behind 'em," TJ answers. "Two transformers."

Transformers are unmarked police cars, they explain, usually Ford Explorers painted in solid colors with no police logo and no lights on top, with two cops in front and two in back.

"Soon as you think about running, they hop right out that motherfucker," TJ says.

"They ready to shoot you, chase you."

"Shoot you, chase you," TJ solemnly repeats. "They're not fucking around."

"You must feel like you're being hunted," I say.

TJ corrects me: "We are hunted. It's a fucking trap."

If "hunted" is your lens for the world, Lewisbey's trial looks like a safari. The prosecutors didn't have a single picture or recording of Lewisbey at the scene of the five gun deals they filmed in the spring of 2012. They had no hard evidence that Lewisbey was engaged in the business of selling guns on any kind of a regular basis. They had no hard evidence that Lewisbey ever sold any of the guns he discussed on Facebook and even some evidence that he wasn't very eager to sell them—when one of his Facebook friends asked if he knew anyone with a shotgun, Lewisbey didn't respond for five months. And if Lewisbey was a legal resident of Indiana, as he claimed to be, he had the legal right to buy as many guns as he wanted. Even moving them to Chicago might be legal because the prevailing court decision held that a person with dual residency in two states could move "a gun" from one state to the other, although the judge and the prosecutor couldn't believe the presiding court intended "a gun" to cover dozens or hundreds of guns. That meant the whole case pivoted on a single point: Was Lewisbey's Indiana ID card valid?

To overcome those obstacles, Parente wove an ornate tapestry of genuine evidence, circumstantial evidence, cooperator testimony, and character assassination. With Facebook posts like "Get rich or die trying" and "I got the game in a knot and you can't untie it," he painted the picture of a thuggish hood with no respect for human life. He didn't mention that many of the lines are actually song lyrics from hip-hop artists like 50 Cent and Gucci Mane, and the investigating officers refused to confirm it on the stand. The prosecutors wanted to keep the focus on Lewisbey's gangster persona. How did he pay for the guns? "Just a big wad of dirty money," one witness said. Did he carry a duffel bag and fill it with guns? "On numerous occasions," the witness said. Another witness said he carried a big bag for a big guy called Big Guy.

"What kind of bag?" Parente asked.

"Like a duffel bag."

He also focused on the cultural distance between the eleven white jurors and the people involved in the gun deals, like the time a cooperating witness testified that he was "waiting on the dude to bring some money."

"Bring the money for what?"

"For the sales of the bangers."

"For the sale of the what?"

"The bangers."

"And that means what again?"

"Guns."

He did it again a few minutes later.

"Holding a banger out?"

"Yes."

"That's a gun?"

"Yes."

To bolster his case, Parente leaned on a series of cooperators, a class of witness that is called the "leading cause of wrongful convictions" by the experts at Northwestern University's Center on Wrongful Convictions. After a massive investigation into the Chicago Police Department in 2016, the Justice Department warned about the CPD's practice of arresting people and refusing to release them until they provide information on a crime. And nobody in Chicago has forgotten Jon Burge, the CPD detective who tortured false confessions out of black suspects for twenty years in a city where the false confession rate is three times the national average.

But cooperators are also the pivot of the majority of criminal trials, and Parente needed them for two of his most crucial arguments. To support the charge that Lewisbey ran his business for four years, he produced a cooperator who said he met Lewisbey at an Indiana gun show in 2008 and saw him buy a lot of guns at some point afterward, date unspecified. To support the charge that Lewisbey was the leader of a conspiracy, he persuaded one of the Gangster Disciples who participated in the gun deals to say he saw Lewisbey take the profits and pay all the helpers.

Finally, Parente brought a man named Daron Jones to the stand. His name was on the application Lewisbey filed to get state residency in Indiana. Lewisbey was childhood friends with Nathanial Thomas, Jones's stepson. At issue was whether Jones had actually signed Lewisbey's application. If he did, Lewisbey's gun purchases would be legal as long as he hadn't knowingly sold them to a felon, a minor, or someone who intended to use them in a crime. And since Indiana didn't require any proof of sale in the case of personal weapons, Parente's prosecution stood to crash right into the gun-show loophole. Lewisbey's criminal liability could vanish if Daron Jones said the signature was his.

Jones said the signature wasn't his but admitted that his memory was sometimes faulty—at which point Parente cut the interview short and called Jones's wife to the stand. She gave him a few useful details—Lewisbey didn't have a key, he only stayed a few months—but flared when he pressed her. "He was allowed to come and spend the night whenever." And when Lewisbey's defense attorney got his turn at Jones, Jones admitted that all the rest of the handwriting on the application was his. He'd filled it out. When Lewisbey's attorney asked if he'd signed it too, Jones hesitated and stumbled over his words.

A handwriting analyst could have resolved the dispute. But the way the legal system is set up, the prosecution and defense aren't really pursuing the truth; they're telling the story most favorable to their client—except in this arena, the quality of their narratives can mean the difference between freedom and a death sentence. Or freedom and seventeen years. And Lewisbey's attorney was about to risk it all with a desperate, swing-for-the-fences plot twist.

For more than forty years, America has been conducting a vast experiment in punishment. To the most troubled neighborhoods in the country, already traumatized by high rates of poverty, mental illness, drug addiction, and violent crime, we have sent zero tolerance and SWAT teams. We banished twice as many people to prison, mostly from those same neighborhoods. Then we doubled that number and doubled it and doubled it again. In the forty-one years from 1973 through 2014, our imprisoned population rose from a low of 200,000 to a peak of 2,224,400. We believed what the politicians told us, that long sentences would keep "superpredators" off the streets, and we tried to ignore the negative effects this policy had on the communities where the prisoners lived before and after—traumatized children, economic insecurity, and the vast army emerging from prisons with a stigma that made finding a job like winning the lottery.

Then the National Research Council analyzed decades of data and declared the whole thing a failure. "Most studies estimate the crime-reducing effect of incarceration to be small," the academy said in *The Growth of Incarceration in the United States*, and there was "no credible evidence of a specific deterrent effect."

The only thing it was really good at was pushing ex-prisoners back into the underground economy of drugs and guns.

For TJ, this was just another example of the distance between his world and the straight world. "Lemme put it in layman's terms for you, John," TJ says. "Politicians and judges and police officers are vegans, and we're the people who eat meat. They say, 'You're wrong, you're killing living creatures,' and we say, 'Okay, maybe it is wrong, but our bodies need the protein.' "

Interrupting one of his many filibusters about the hypocrisy and corruption of police officers, I ask him if he ever met a good cop. "Good police?" he says. "Fuck no!"

"If they catch a guy with weed," his friend says, "they'll tell him, 'Give me a gun, or give me a crib to hit,' then they'll go hit that crib and tell 'em the dude gave up their crib."

"That'll start a gang war," TJ says.

But now it's time to get back to hustling. For TJ's friend, that means "bitches, streets, finessing." TJ has a few more walnuts of weed to sell before we head up to Chinatown, where the Gangster Disciples collected a duffel bag full of Lewisbey's guns. He's going to show me the underpass where the deal went down.

As he makes his drops, TJ starts to wonder if this tour is worth his time. He finds a spot to stop—backing in, as always—and pulls up stories on his phones. "150 Guns Stolen at Norfolk Southern Railway Yard" ... "Another Rail-Car Theft of Semi-Automatic Rifles" ... "Andrew Shelton Stole More than 100 pistols." He also could have mentioned the two licensed gun shops just outside the city line, Chuck's Gun Shop and Midwest Sporting Goods. They pumped more crime guns into the city than any other single source, about 12 percent of the total.

This is what TJ means when he says, "Shit happens every day," his shorthand for the experience of violence as a moment-to-moment possibility. He's saying that politicians and police and suburbanites can glance at the statistics or watch the horror stories on TV, but none of that matters in the real world. Spikes in crime don't matter. Crackdowns don't matter. People in poor neighborhoods have turned to crime since civilization began, which means they've been subject to spikes and crackdowns for just as long. In Chicago, that means using force on black people almost ten times as often as on whites and getting away with it—only 2 percent of the 30,000 complaints about police abuse filed in the previous five years were sustained, and only 2 percent of those triggered any kind of punishment. The system is so stacked against victims of police abuse, the review board is forbidden from considering any previous complaints against an officer, "even where those incidents may include serious misconduct." The real purpose of Chicago's complaint system, the Justice Department concluded in a January 13 report, was "misleading the public into thinking that accountability has been achieved."

Cruising through Chinatown, TJ points out the underpass, which is right next to the Chinese Community Center. The projects across the street are like a small city behind a fence, everybody living on top of one another with all their sore spots rubbing. "Ain't no rules," TJ says. "Anything goes."

For a while, police wouldn't even go in the gate.

Strike one was his refusal to cooperate. Strike two was demanding a jury trial, an option that has almost disappeared—only 2 percent of Americans who face criminal charges insist on a trial. So Lewisbey was already a candidate for Most Annoying Defendant before he decided to testify in his own case, a dangerous option that most defense attorneys vigorously discourage. Then he told the jury that he wasn't running guns because he was such a successful weed dealer that he didn't need the money. The headline in the *Chicago Sun-Times* captured the public reaction: "Defendant Denies Selling Guns to Gangs: Trust Me, I'm a Drug Dealer."

Applying TJ's metaphor of the trap, this would be the last turn of the key. Lewisbey had just turned twenty-three. He didn't have any money. Most of all, he had no way of knowing that the lawyer his mother had hired was under investigation (and would soon be indicted) for coaching witnesses. So he took his lawyer's advice and repeated the answers the guy dreamed up for him, or so he says—repeated phone calls failed to get a response from the lawyer, Beau Brindley. That was perjury, and he deserved to be punished for it, he admits, but he was driven by another beginner's mistake—there were things he wanted to get off his chest. With the indignation of an innocent man, he told me that Daron Jones went to the DMV with him to file that application. The DMV lady was standing right there when he signed it. That's mandatory. A legal resident with all his IDs has to go to the DMV office with you and sign the application in front of them. Why would he fill it out and not sign it? Why didn't anyone ask?

Did he buy and sell guns? Hell yes, he said. He did it for Worm that fateful weekend because he could get better deals and didn't see anything wrong with it. Private dealers sell nearly half the guns sold in the United States, he said. "I seen it done every day at gun shows."

Parente glimpsed an opening. What about the guns at issue? Didn't he care what a customer might do with a gun he sold?

Lewisbey hesitated and made the most fateful beginner's mistake of all—an honest answer: "I mean, no."

Parente lunged. "You didn't care? If he wanted to go rob something, you're just going to get him the gun? You don't care what he does with the gun you're going to get him?"

Sensing a trap, Lewisbey doubled down. "I mean, is it really—am I supposed to care?"

Could there be more vivid evidence of a criminal mind?

The jury took only a few hours to convict him. Celebrations of the triumph of justice followed. "This is one of the most significant gun-trafficking cases we have prosecuted and one that effectively ended a steady supply of potentially lethal weapons from Indiana to Chicago," the U.S. Attorney declared. Looking forward, the *Tribune* editorial board called for tough justice: "Part of restoring law to lawless streets is enforcing serious penalties on lawbreakers."

When the time for judgment came, the U.S. Attorney sent the judge a fiery sentencing memorandum calling for a series of "enhancements" to the ten-year maximum: four points for knowingly trafficking guns to an individual who intended to use them for unlawful purposes; another four for leading a conspiracy of five or more persons; four more for using or possessing a firearm in connection with a felony offense; and a final four for trying to obstruct justice with the "get put up" warning to Worm and his lies about being a big weed dealer. But the memo's supporting arguments revealed the weakness of the most damaging charges against Lewisbey. The U.S. Attorney said Lewisbey started buying "duffel bags full of guns" in 2008, a claim based entirely on an ambiguous statement from a single cooperator. Parente based a charge that

Lewisbey bought more than 200 firearms, the number that triggered a 10 percent increase in his base sentence, on nothing more than an assumption: "A person who can so easily obtain forty-three guns in a weekend certainly has the knowledge, ability, and resources to buy a lot of guns." He even turned Lewisbey's stable life and clean record into an indictment.

"The defendant was in a remarkable position to actually make something of his life. He had no criminal background. He had a strong relationship with his parents. He had a background in athletics and was attending college. He had opportunity after opportunity in front of him. But instead of capitalizing on that, he exploited it. He used his status as a non-felon to be the guy who could get the guns for the felons."

In conclusion, Parente asked for the longest sentence the law would allow. "Given the current climate of violence and destruction in Chicago," he said, "the message must be sent that supplying this city with undocumented, unregistered, untraceable, illegal guns will not be tolerated."

The judge agreed, accepting all but two of the enhancement points. In his sentencing statement, he dismissed the idea that a first offense for a nonviolent crime called for mercy. Lewisbey "had a part" in the city's plague of bloodshed, he said. "When you provide the tools, you are setting in motion a series of events, and you can't just play ostrich and stick your head in the sand and say, 'That's not my doing.' "

So the message was sent. But how was it received?

Because human justice is a battle between competing narratives and the media usually loves competing narratives, it's odd that Lewisbey's back story failed to attract a single reporter. Nobody talked to Lewisbey's football coaches or teachers. Nobody talked to his friends or his minister, Dr. Odell Sterling. Although his mother attended every day of the trial, nobody interviewed her or took any interest in finding out how Lewisbey grew up. His role in the drama was fixed—he was the thug with the big wad of money and the duffel bag full of guns.

But he wasn't a thug. The Lewisbey family lives in a planned community well outside the troubles of Chicago. Their house has a two-story living room faced in glass, a two-story cathedral arch above the front door, a two-story garage, and adventurous Miami-Beach-meets-Afro-Modernism decor. Lewisbey's stepfather is a steady earner who manages a local graveyard. His mother is a patient-claims administrator at a hospital and avid church member. "No Ebonics in the house" is just one of her rules.

Her name is Felesa Melvin. When she greets me in the driveway, she's dressed like a New Yorker in stretchy black leggings and a matching black top. She leads the way to the dining table and tells another story the jury never heard. Four of her friends had their sons killed by guns. Tracy's was a random drive-by, Amy's son was trying to break up a fight, the other two she isn't sure what happened. But the point is, David knew those kids. He grieved for them. "The monster they painted my baby as, he was not that monster."

At the trial the prosecutor made sure the jury knew Melvin owned a gun and her husband had a felony, casting two more shadows on the family. But her husband's felony was for sleeping with a seventeen-year-old girl when he was eighteen, and the gun was a .22 David gave her because he wanted her to be safe—she hated guns. And that was just like the stories they told about David. The big wad of cash? All singles. He'd wrap a twenty around it so he looked like he had something.

The Facebook stuff was horrible to see, all that gangster rap and "bitches" this and that. David wasn't raised to be disrespectful to women. But he posted other things too. She opens her laptop to show me some: "There is nothing God cannot do, so pray big, dream big, believe big and expect big ... count your blessings ... everything is a blessing." But none of that came up in court either.

For her, the worst moment was when Daron Jones and Shari Lewis said David didn't really stay with Nathanial, she says. The boys had been friends since ninth grade. "For the family to lie like that—he had the garage-door code and a key." But the system does that to people. It has so much power, it can turn them against each other.

Up in her son's bedroom, his pocket litter is still on the bureau. That's his sneaker collection in the box. His football helmet's still in the closet. His prom suit's in there too, along with a paper pyramid he made in middle school. She lingers for a few moments, feeling his presence and his absence.

The way she sees it now, David got caught up in something his friends were doing. "Dave was hanging around some bad people," she says, letting out a resigned sigh. Worm, for example. Worm was the first thing the police asked about when they made the arrest, and Worm was in the Gangster Disciples too. He and David had been friends since they were thirteen or fourteen. She wonders sometimes how much of that Facebook stuff David really believed. Did he get caught up in all that hoodlum glamour? Did the world's injustice make him bitter?

But then she stops to reconsider. No, bad was too strong a word. Worm had a sweet side. He was respectful. He always pulled up his saggy-ass pants before coming into the house. "Kids like that come from so many problems," she says. "They go to the streets for love."

Was Lewisbey guilty? At the very least, he knew where those guns were going and what they might do. And even though the law against making commercial sales without a license is rarely enforced, Lewisbey was probably guilty of that too. And maybe Parente was right; maybe he just saw an opportunity and took it. But the way Lewisbey sees it, he shouldn't even have been charged with commercial sales. Gary Barrett did the exact same thing. He was the fifty-three-year-old Sears manager who was listed in Lewisbey's phone book under "Gary Glocks," the one who sold Lewisbey forty-three guns on that fateful April weekend in 2012. He was also the only "person of interest" in the case who wasn't a black guy from Chicago, and the only one who didn't get arrested—funny how that happens, right?

Everything else he did was legal, Lewisbey insists. He could buy and sell as many guns as he wanted under Indiana law as long as his state ID was legal. He could drive them from state to state too. It was even legal to sell them to Worm, who didn't have a felony at the time. The whole thing was cut-and-dry and no big deal. "Worm wanted firearms. I knew Gary Barrett. Worm gave me his money for the firearms."

Visiting time is over now. The prisoners and guests walk down a painted exit line until it splits in two directions. As we approach the splitting point, Lewisbey says he's not letting things bother him too much. He's been meeting interesting people. He quit smoking weed. "I'm studying real estate, Wall Street, getting into currency trading—I like the pound, yen, the Swiss franc. I keep myself busy."

But in some of the photos he sent from prison, he's standing with a man TJ identified as a notorious gang lord. There's also a strain of militant thinking in his letters, bits of Muslim wisdom, and bitter comments about unequal justice. And the question that sealed his fate festers in his mind. Did Gary Glocks care what happened to the guns he sold? Do gun-shop owners care? Do gun manufacturers care? Does the NRA care? Do politicians care? If you have a part in killings because you provide the tools, why aren't all of them in prison for seventeen years?

David "Big Man" Lewisbey will be out when he's thirty-seven.

As TJ steers the car around the potholes of a scrappy back road near the Indiana border, he explains the difference between trust and loyalty. "You can trust someone to do a deal with them. Loyalty is you'll stand with a person no matter what. So trust and loyalty are related, but they're two different things."

The point is, he'll show me some things based on trust, but he won't show me others—unless we get our relationship closer to loyalty.

He pulls into my hotel parking lot and reverses into a parking space. "The question I'm asking is, how much is it worth to you?" he says. "Are you willing to take a risk?"

I'd like to know more about the nature of the risk, I say.

He'll explain upstairs, he says.

He's in the easy chair now, kicked back with his feet up on the ottoman, looking relaxed and in control.

"You'd have to do something," he says.

"What would I have to do?"

"What I can show you isn't in Chicago," he says. "It's in Indiana."

Figuring it out isn't hard. I'm just like David, a mainstream guy with a clean record and a rented car. "You want me to drive?"

He nods.

"Across the border?"

He nods again. "It's safe," he says. "We know how to hide things."

"Unless there's an informant," I say.

"There's no informants," he snaps. "I guarantee that."

So the moment arrives. It's not about laws, it's just yes or no, in or out, and yes is a down payment on loyalty. Yes is boldness in the face of danger and standing up like a man. No is being a pussy and missing out. So what is it? Are you willing to take a risk? Do you want to learn how to hustle? Even I can't help being tempted by the mixture of adventure and opportunity. For a good story and general enhancement of my legend, it might be worth it. So what would I say if I had brown skin, listened to defiant hip-hop, and had childhood friends who grew up to be the Gangster Disciples?

And just like that, the moment passes.

"It's too late," TJ says.

That's his final lesson. The tests of brotherhood and courage aren't open book, and they're not graded on a curve. They're snap tests, and they're always pass-fail. Until I can feel that feeling from the inside, I have no right to judge.

As we turn onto a more rural road, he relaxes and starts asking questions about how people get ahead in the straight world. The whole enterprise seems to puzzle him. It's like something buzzing around his head that he can't see. "I am trying to better myself," he says. Right now, he's trying to get into a building-trades union. Long term, he's thinking real estate or maybe a franchise. "I don't share that with many people because a lot of them shit on your dreams."

But even when he becomes an upright citizen, he says, some things will never change. "I'm still going to keep my fucking guns. You never know when you might need them."

THE LATIN KINGS

After Latin King leader King Blood was convicted of ordering twelve murders and seventeen attempted murders, his successor, King Tone, took over and declared peace. The Latin Kings were going straight, he declared. The club would incorporate, get wives and kids involved, make alliances with local politicians. But then King Wiz was stabbed. That's when the mayhem really got started.

King Wiz has two holes in his head. One bullet went through his brain and came out the other side. The other exploded his eye into a bulging red pulp. Right now, a plastic plug holds his mouth open to make room for the tubes that are keeping him alive.

King Tone approaches the bedside and puts two fingers in Wiz's open hand.

"This is King Tone," he says. "I love you, man."

The life monitors beat out the time.

There's a crust of dried tears running down the side of Wiz's head, a tattoo of a crown above his heart—the symbol of the Almighty Latin King Queen Nation.

"You going to be all right, all right?" Tone says. "We'll all be waiting for you, all right?"

The monitors pulse.

"I'll be back," Tone says. "Be strong."

Then he goes downstairs, to the lobby of the hospital, where the kid everyone thinks shot Wiz is waiting—waiting to see whether Tone will let him live.

All last fall, we read the lurid headlines: "Latin King Boss Ordered Savage Killings From Jail. Hispanic Goodfellas Formed Murder Inc." Virtually unknown in New York just five years ago, the Latin Kings were now routinely described as the most notorious street gang in the city. In a federal courtroom in downtown Manhattan, government prosecutors described the Latin Kings as a highly organized "criminal enterprise" responsible for twelve murders and seventeen attempted murders. Despite the gruesome details—one victim had his head and hands cut off, his corpse set afire in a bathtub—the gory headlines actually underplayed the scope of the government's case: In the end, nearly fifty Latin Kings were convicted of murder, attempted murder, or assault — among them Luis Felipe, a.k.a. King Blood, the thirty-four-year-old founder and "Inca" of the New York Kings.

Now the Latin Kings had a new leader, a thirty-year-old former crack addict named Antonio Fernandez. For the past six months, Fernandez—known as King Tone—and his Kings had been appearing at rallies across the city. They'd marched against police brutality, marched against gentrification, made common cause with the family of Anthony Baez, whose death at the hands of police officer Francis Livoti enraged much of New York's Latino community—and police would later accuse them of subcontracting (for $5,000) a retaliatory sniper attack against police captain Steven Plavnick. They had formed alliances with a group of left-to-radical community leaders like Al Sharpton, Vicente "Panama" Alba, and Richie Perez. They even had a priest in their corner, Father Luis Barrios of Harlem's St. Mary's Episcopal Church.

All through Felipe's trial, King Tone brought a squad of fresh-faced young Kings and Queens to federal court to support him. Identifiable by brown skin and black and yellow clothes—black and gold are the Latin Kings' colors—the young Kings and Queens seemed intimidated by the grandeur of the federal courtroom: the twenty-five-foot ceilings, the mahogany paneling, the whole somber ritual of justice. One young Queen wore a sweatshirt decorated with a teddy-bear applique and took detailed notes in a schoolgirl's three-ring binder.

In court, I tried to figure out which King was King Tone. Was it the watchful man in the leather jacket? The somber guy with the deep pockmarks? The last one on my list was a goofy-looking guy who looked white but dressed ghetto. Pigeon-toed and bowlegged, his hair shaved up the sides of his head in a hip-hop fade, he walked around in a puffy black-and-yellow coat looking like a homeboy bumblebee. One day, I saw him grinning at a spectator. "I came to see my father," he said, pointing to Felipe. "Would you believe that's my father?"

That was King Tone. For weeks, he and the other Kings listened as the state's witnesses testified. One day, defense attorney Lawrence Feitell asked a prosecution witness named Nelson Torres what it was like to kill. Torres had been the Kings' number three man in Brooklyn—the "warlord."

"When you shoot people, do you get nervous?"

"I get a rush," Torres answered.

"Have you ever been referred to as the Demolition Man?" Feitell continued.

"Yeah. That meant when I hit somebody, they're going to go down."

"You look on that as a compliment, do you not?"

"I hit hard," Torres answered.

And that was the *defense*. The prosecutors presented the Kings as a bizarre killer cult with a fetish for rules and regulations. They had a particular respect for the written word, keeping individual "bibles" of Kingist teachings, which range from their history to advice on pregnancy. Even the TOS—"terminate on sight"—orders were written down. As were pardons: "I, King Blaze, supreme crown of Rhode Island, use the power of my crown to declare a stop to the TOS on Pete Rock."

Felipe's letters—thousands of them—were the heart of the trial. They were stunningly incriminating, a prosecutor's dream. "About Mousey—that dude is a real threat to our nation, and before he do any more damage he must be terminated," he wrote in one. Mousey had dared to rewrite the King lessons. In another: "If by this time next year he ain't done yet, I'll do him myself and it will be a pleasure."

It was a classic open-and-shut case, except for one thing: The prosecutors had charged the Kings under the RICO racketeering act, and it quickly became clear that there wasn't much money in being a King—no big drug schemes, extortion, or prostitution. The King constitution frowned on the use of "hard" drugs, and Felipe himself depended on irregular $20 donations to buy stamps.

So why all the killing?

And why were all these kids visiting the courtroom every day?

One Saturday, I went to Brooklyn to meet King Tone. As the El rumbled by ten feet away, we sat on the steps of a graffiti-marked building just off Knickerbocker Avenue. For the next three hours, Tone told me how he and his Supreme Team took control of the Kings, ousted the most unruly members, and made peace with rival street organizations. The Latin Kings are notorious for fighting in packs, but Tone said he'd banned 911s (the King calls to battle). The Kings were also famous for giving "physicals" to members who try to quit, but Tone had created a Golden Gate form to release disgruntled members peacefully. The King constitution ordered Kings to obey their Crowns without question, but Tone changed it so they only had to obey the orders that were "righteous." He filed to make the Kings a legal corporation. He got wives and children involved and changed the gang's name to the Almighty King *Queen* Nation. He even put together a press kit.

The prosecutors told me this was nothing but a smoke screen, that the Kings had done the misunderstood-youth act for reporters before. And at times, Tone's story did seem too good to be true. "I teach these kids how to study," he insisted. "I taught them when you go home, turn off the Atari, turn off the damn TV, and you give yourself three hours of quality time. And now they come through flying colors with their schools."

But Tone had charm. At times, he slipped into a preacher's rhythms, often ending a story by turning his face into a kind of smiling riot mask: So-there-you-have-it, my brother. Squint and he became a venerable ancient narrating the traditions of his tribe.

And many of his answers seemed quite honest. Why did the Kings decide to go public? "I knew Blood's jury would be picked in New York, and I knew we needed to change our image fast."

What about the police insistence that there were still Kings involved in crime?

"There must be," he agreed. "Just like there still must be cops out there still doing corrupt things."

Tone didn't even try to convince me Felipe was innocent. He described life in prison, twenty-three-hour-a-day lockdown with nothing but a pen and paper and a strange kind of long-distance power. "I believe he lost ... sanity," Tone said.

But that didn't change the Kings' loyalty—if anything, it intensified it. "People don't understand," Tone continued. "I'm not loyal to him. I'm loyal to the dream."

What was that dream? What was worth killing for? Dying for?

As Tone tried to explain, a living answer walked by. He looked barely twenty, as handsome as a Disney prince. His name was King Wiz.

"Show him your belly," Tone ordered.

Wiz pulled up his T-shirt: a row of Band-Aids climbed out of his pants to his ribs.

Just two weeks earlier, Tone explained, Wiz had almost died for the Kings. As Tone told the story, it began when the Kings got a tip that an ex-King named Jose was telling people that Tone was a snitch. On the streets, snitches tend to have a short life expectancy, so Tone sent three men over to Jose's house to talk to him—unarmed. He sent Wiz because Wiz was one of Jose's best friends. But the cops stopped them and searched them, and by the time they got to Jose's house it was after midnight and one thing led to another and a King hit Jose and Jose pulled out a knife. Tone says Wiz took twenty stitches and almost died.

Which left Tone with a decision to make: "Do I go the old school—you know, kill this guy or whatever?"

While Tone was making plans, the cops picked up Jose. They charged him with attempted murder and tried to get him to turn on Tone, offering him clemency and relocation. When Jose refused, they put him in a jail cell with "seven Latin guys that are supposed to be Kings."

Five stab wounds later, Jose was ready to start a war. And he had some very well-armed friends.

But the point Tone was trying to make was that he didn't go the old school. Instead, he held a peace meeting with Jose: "I told him that I was wrong, because I shouldn't have sent my men at that time of night to create such a misfortune, and you relate to all your little drug dealers that you were wrong for stabbing my brother. And it's ended!"

Clearly, Tone wanted me to see him as a peacemaker, struggling to keep a lid on violence that was always on the verge of boiling over. He was admitting that despite all their we've-reformed publicity, Kings were still confronting their enemies in the middle of the night. Even now, he continued, some Kings didn't think Jose's five shallow stab wounds punishment enough. "These guys don't want somebody they think is going to crumble every time there's a problem," he said. "So I got to win battles ... without wars. And it's a thin line, 'cause sometimes it's, 'Fuck Tone, we're the Latin Kings!' "

The Almighty Latin King Nation began in Chicago in the 1940s, one of dozens of street-and-prison gangs in the city. What made the Kings different was their mixture of intense discipline and revolutionary politics with a homemade religion called Kingism, adding idealism and a boot-camp rigor to the usual gang camaraderie—a potent mixture for troubled ghetto kids whose lives lacked structure and hope.

Luis Felipe was one of those kids. Born in Cuba in 1962, he smuggled himself into Florida on a fishing boat, drifted north, and joined the Kings in Chicago. He then moved to the Bronx, where he was convicted of manslaughter in the death of his girlfriend—he claims they were struggling over a gun—and sent to Collins Correctional Facility in upstate New York.

It was there, in 1986, that Felipe started the New York branch of the Kings. As he described it later in letters and an interview, he began with two friends named Chito and Diablo, telling them about the King ideals. At the time, black gangs dominated the prisons, making life difficult for Latinos. A week later, Felipe had nine followers, sixty more two months after that. Then a Black Muslim jumped a King, and "the shit hit the fence in the middle of the summer of '87 in Collins #2 yard," as Felipe later wrote. "The Almighty Latin Kings nation went to their first real war in the state of New York!"

In an effort to break up the nascent gang, prison officials transferred the Kings to different prisons—where they spread the new faith even faster. By the early 1990s, the Kings were starting to emerge from prison onto the streets. In 1992, an anthropology professor named Ric Curtis was working out of a storefront in Bushwick studying street culture. "That summer, a bunch of guys went into prison, and the next summer they all came out Latin Kings," he told me. "It was that quick." Ironically, Curtis attributed the rise of the Latin Kings to the rising incarceration rates of the drug war—a literal return of the repressed.

Around the same time, a Housing Police officer approached Elizabeth Glazer, then head of the U.S. Attorney's Organized Crime unit, telling her of a peculiar rooftop murder in the Bronx. "It was done in what seemed essentially to be a ritual manner," she recalled recently. "He had his arms crossed, black and gold beads, shot in the back of the head." Federal investigators started looking into it and soon noticed a pattern of similar unsolved murders.

Before long, the FBI, the NYPD, the Housing Police, and the Corrections Department began cooperating to develop a RICO case against the Kings, each contributing a piece of the puzzle. Guards in Attica steamed open Felipe's mail, and the FBI and police linked the letters to actions on the street. "It was evolving each day," said Steve Cohen, the assistant U.S. Attorney who took charge of the investigation. "The cops tell you they saw 150 Kings at a meeting in the Bronx, and you start to say, hey, we're dealing with some large numbers."

Eventually they put it together: King Russ, killed for running from a fight; King Lite, killed for kissing Felipe's "wife"; King Ace, killed for accusing other Kings of stealing; King Lex, killed for warning King Ace he was marked for death ... the list goes on. "The most disturbing thing was this very public cruelty," Cohen said. "They profess love, yet they think it's fun to watch this brother get beat to a pulp in front of them. It breeds this sense that they're their own nation, that Kings and Queens are above the law."

By the summer of 1994, they were ready to start making arrests.

Kings greet each other by throwing their crown—a three-fingered slap to the shoulder—and hugging each other tight. "Giving love," they call it. Which means there's always a lot of hugging at Charas, a community center on the Lower East Side where the Kings hold many of their meetings. One night, I watched them clean out a classroom, carrying desks and chairs past a blackboard covered in graffiti.

When the room was empty, forty-five Kings formed a circle.

"*Amor de rey*," someone said. Love of the king.

And the whole group shouted it back: "*Amor de rey!*"

Then the Kings knelt—right knee pointing down to hell and left knee up to Heaven. "My Father that made us, yesterday today and tomorrow, Almighty Father, king of kings ..."

"*Amor de rey!*"

Finally, Tone entered the circle. Kings bowed to him, kissing their crowns. After a warning about the media—"Every little thing you do is being watched, so watch everything you do, you understand?"—Tone launched into a sermon on the three wise kings who brought gifts to baby Jesus. A rousing mixture of inspiration and social resentment, it drifted from praise of the "warrior spirit" of Jesus to the evil of racist cops to an attack on America itself:

"They lost touch with reality. That's why they got homeless, that's why their biggest industry is prisons—because they no longer under God. They think they're above him. And that's where we kick them in the butt, say, 'We're not above God but we're not under you, America, and your nasty-ass teachings, and your foolish plan to put me in jail and make you rich. Kings are the ones who are going to make a change! They can call us crazy, they can say what they want, but we're going to keep pumping until everybody wakes up and recognizes who we are!"

"Amor de rey!"

The dreams were all about pride. The Kings and Queens talked about distributing food to the homeless, about respecting one another, about going to school and keeping steady jobs. They gave book reports on Puerto Rican history. Inside their circles, they weren't just despised street punks but Kings, members of a nation "360 degrees strong." And their nation gave them recognition—as one King leader told me, "I work at this low-level flunky job, but I lead thousands of people through the Nation."

But one night Tone and I bumped into another young King with trouble on his mind. We were on the M train going from Brooklyn to Manhattan. "I'm going to go in with you to the D.A.'s office," Tone said, shouting over the subway noise. "If you don't leave, I won't leave, either."

The young King—a sleepy, amiable guy named Era—nodded and grinned but he seemed very uncomfortable. Later I learned that he'd witnessed a shootout last March that left a King called Bishop Jr. dead. The beef started when Era saw Bishop Jr.'s girlfriend with another man. When Era told him, "He started crying—he said, 'I don't believe she did this to me, especially in my own house.' " The next day, Era and Bishop Jr. and some other Kings went over to take Bishop Jr.'s baby daughter for a visit—King brotherhood in action.

But the new boyfriend pulled out a gun. Moments later, Era was holding his dying friend as the shooter ran down the fire escape. "If we had a gun, to tell you the truth, he would have been dead," Era said.

Afterward, the Kings refused to cooperate with the police. Era went to Puerto Rico. Now he was back, and Tone was trying to persuade him to talk to the Brooklyn D.A. "I'm going to give them the key witness they need, and I'm going to see if Kings' blood is cheap again," he told me.

But could the Kings really move from street justice to straight justice? Would Era really go through with it?

"He will," Tone said, "because I told him to, and I'm his Inca."

Antonio Fernandez was born in 1966 in Brooklyn, son of a bread-delivery man and a mother so religious she hasn't had a single cigarette or drink her whole life. He grew up in a single-family house, played baseball, and got good grades. Then he discovered crack. He loved it, everything about it, "the taste, the mint that numbs your tongue, the rush of the speedball." Before long, he was joining baby gangs and dabbling in petty crime. He repeated ninth grade four years in a row. He stole his mother's wedding ring to pay for drugs.

When Tone was about nineteen, he found Jesus. He joined the Victory Outreach Church and spent four years preaching in the streets. "He was one of those guys who really fall in love with God," said Victory Outreach pastor Larry Arreola.

Then Tone started smoking crack again, and a bust for possession landed him on Rikers Island. There he started fighting to "build up my dignity and my respect," as he put it. One morning four guys caught him in a deserted aisle and attacked him with razors. "When I got to the nurse, she said, 'Man, a little bit over and they would have cut your heart.' " On his release, Tone quickly got himself arrested again. But this time, he opted into the Shock program, six months of character-building boot camp, and it worked—he gave up crack and came out to a regular job as mailroom supervisor at an advertising agency.

By then he was also a dedicated Latin King. Kingism kept him off crack, gave him something to live for. Soon he became bodyguard to King Teardrop, the nation's number two man and later one of the government's prize catches. After the federal indictments cleaned away much of his competition, Tone took over. During this period, tension was building between the Kings and another prison-and-street group called the Netas. As Neta leader Green Eyes told me later: "Everybody was running around 'cause my guys thought Tone was going to get to me first, and his guys thought I was going to get to Tone first." They finally came face-to-face two years ago in a garage in Bushwick, two small armies in "full war gear"—and decided to make peace. Eventually, with the help of an ex-gangster turned social activist named Hector Torres, the Kings started the United Families, a citywide gang coalition. Peace was at hand.

In May of 1995, Tone was arrested for possession of a handgun. The arrest was peculiar—a cop searched him carefully enough to find (allegedly) marijuana in his pocket but didn't find the .38 in his jeans until he searched him again in the station house. Insisting he was framed, Tone made bail, only to have his parole revoked on the pending gun charge. After a campaign by the Kings to get him out, famed left-wing attorney Ron Kuby agreed to take his case, and with Latin Kings packing the courtroom—100 to 200 at a time—Kuby beat the charges.

Then Tone was indicted on *federal* gun charges—a third arrest for the same .38 special. This time, the judge's decision was withering: "It is extremely difficult to believe that the same officer [who found a small bag of marijuana] could have missed a bulky .38 caliber revolver hidden in the Defendant's pants," she wrote.

When Tone finally came out of jail last February, he emerged with a new political fire. Within days, he attended a march against police brutality. He got a job registering voters. He reorganized the Kings, bringing in young leaders without prison records. And he began attending the trial of Francis Livoti, the police officer accused of killing a Puerto Rican named Anthony Baez, becoming so close to Baez's mother, Iris, that when Livoti was found innocent, she sent everyone else away and broke down in his arms. "That's a day I'll never forget in my life," Tone told me. "It gave me so much more to fight for."

In the street outside the courtroom that day, Baez collapsed from grief. As hundreds of riot-gear-clad cops watched, Tone and the Kings surrounded her in one of their ritual circles until the ambulance came. Some reporters and police officers on the scene said they heard Latin Kings swearing revenge. A week later, when Captain Plavnick was shot in the back by a sniper, anonymous police sources immediately began blaming the Latin Kings.

As the weeks passed, I began to like Tone. He was funny. Sometimes he had an almost beatific sweetness. But I kept thinking that he'd been a King through the bad times, bodyguard to Teardrop. He couldn't be completely innocent.

And he wasn't. "There was rec time—once a week when they could drink a beer and beat up a kid and feel good," Tone said. "We used to come to a place like this"—he pointed out the car window to a pool hall—"pick any nigger, and all his friends wouldn't move, and start beating him, and nobody tell you nothing. It's power, my brother. These people were all about power."

And you, Tone?

"Truth is, I know what it is to give a physical," he said. "I know what it is to have a brother with his hands in his pockets and hurt him. But the thing that always made me different was, I was a cheater when it came to hurting my brother: I'm hitting him and I'm looking at the guy—*Please act like it's hurting*. But no, I never killed anybody for this nation."

What stopped him?

"I had my morals, and it scalded."

So why bodyguard for Teardrop?

"I had to work my way up."

"In the Nation?"

"Yeah."

But *why*?

Tone seemed a bit exasperated. "I had to take it *over*," he said.

But why not just get a job, raise a family?

Tone smiled. "This never would have happened. Fucking history wouldn't have been made."

I couldn't help laughing. History?

"Believe me," Tone insisted. "They talk about the fucking Young Lords—wait till they talk about the Kings twenty years from now. What I'm breeding is a true revolution. I believe ten years from now the Kings will be a big, big force, and you'll step to Kings and say, 'Ain't none of you from broken homes and out of jail? Why are you Kings?' And they'd say, 'Well, my father was a King ...' "

And he smiled his riot smile.

Tone is never alone. Most days, he's accompanied by Hector Torres, who's put his other activism on hold to become Tone's full-time cheerleader and adviser. By nighttime, Tone usually hooks up with King Noel, a somber young man who works security at a law firm and spent years as a New Age "rebirther" before turning to Kingism.

Also, Queen Rosi, a bright young woman who works at a bank and has a degree in child development from Fordham. Or King Lalo, a watchful twenty-eight-year-old who boxed Golden Gloves in the army before going to Rikers on a gun-possession charge. (Over pizza one day, Lalo told me that his title—Warlord—had been changed to Peacemaker.) Or King Mission, a high-school kid so well-behaved that when I gave him a ride one day, he first called his mother for permission to get in a stranger's car.

Most of the time, we went to rallies of one kind or another—the Kings are regulars on the protest circuit. At every church and school, we ran into Iris Baez and the grief-stricken mothers of Parents Against Police Brutality. Whenever she saw Tone, Baez hugged him. The Kings had been a rock and a comfort, she told me: "They're good kids once you get to know them."

One day, Tone told me that a brother named King Wiz had been shot in the Bronx. Wiz was twenty-eight, liked to race cars, a generous guy who always had time to help people out. The shooter was rumored to be his best friend. After the shooting, he had been seen on the street wearing a bullet-proof vest, but the cops had just questioned him and let him go. "So now everybody wants me to do something," Tone sighed. "Even the cops—that's why they let him go. So King Tone would have to act."

A few days later, we went up to the hospital to see Wiz, and when we came back down from intensive care with the image of that exploded eye in our heads—you couldn't *not* think of it—we found the kid everyone was sure fired the shots. He was small and dark brown, dressed in a puffy jacket and knit hat. He had come—with his mother—to visit Wiz.

As Kings took up point, Tone approached him. Wiz's mother followed, anger and suspicion on her face. The two mothers and two men went into a huddle, and after a few minutes Tone's voice rose loud enough to hear from ten feet away: "I'm not scared of you motherfuckers. Instead of you hiding, why don't you go out and find out who did it?"

Once again, Tone had chosen not to go to the old school. But five minutes after it was over, the kid still looked scared.

Felipe's attorney rested without mounting a defense. In his summation, he leaned heavily on the revolutionary rhetoric of the 1960s—Felipe was really "a resister, a visionary," and the state was so "threatened" by his power that it was prepared to "carpet-bomb" the Kings.

The jury took five hours. As the foreman prepared to read the verdict, U.S. marshals flooded into the courtroom. But the Kings took it quietly, giving Blood an intense *amor de rey* as the Marshals led him back to his cell. Then they went downstairs and formed their circle on the sidewalk. Tone wept as he led them in prayer.

A block away, at the U.S. Attorney's building, prosecutor Rich Zabel walked in beaming, "Guilty on all counts," he announced. Congratulations rang out.

Upstairs, the prosecutors talked about the case. Although they tried to be evenhanded, admitting the Latin Kings' emphasis on cultural heritage and Puerto Rican solidarity, they seemed half-hearted. Neither they nor the FBI agents I talked to later saw much chance the Kings could ever change. They were bad guys, and that was that. Didn't their poverty indicate at least an effort at virtue? "They don't have a lot of money by the standards of major drug gangs," Steve Cohen said grudgingly, "but they had enough to buy guns." Those fresh-faced kids showing up in court every day? "It's disturbing that these fresh-faced kids are coming in to pay tribute to a man who had committed these terrible crimes."

And the religion?

"It's *Lord of the Flies* with automatic weapons."

The sacred documents of the Kings are supposed to be secret, but Tone finally agreed to let me see them. Cohen showed me others. Kept in individual "bibles"—usually three-ring binders a kid might take to school—most of the rules and lessons are very idealistic: "A member must speak the truth at all times. ... A member must not lust for pleasure in another member's spouse. ... A member must not steal." There are moments of real poetry—one lesson refers to "the power of indestructible things to make this broken world whole again"—and a constant, almost plaintive emphasis on racial pride:

"Latinos are always willing to die with dignity and honor for our Latin race. ... Latin Kings are people with morals and principles, with honor, dignity, and pride ..."

The dark side is a scary militarism: "A King must never deny his superiors ... never hesitate against an enemy of the nation. ... Traitors must die at all costs. ... If by death is the only way you will keep and honor our code of silence, you will die."

Both sides of Kingism came together the day I went to the Schuylkill federal penitentiary to see Luis Felipe. He came into the visiting room shackled and hid his hands under the table. He had a twitch, blinking his eyes hard two or three times in succession all through the interview. As he spoke in a street-rough voice of his love for history and his Latino brothers, he seemed to be a man of great will beaten to an explosive, wary stillness. When I asked him about the murders, he made excuses. But finally he just shrugged. "What I did, I did," he said. "The people that died were the ones that were destroying this nation."

Tone says the threat of war is the only way he can keep the peace. Say a kid comes up with a gun and starts running his mouth—Tone would just have to get in his face. "You want to fight—you want a war? Now the kid thinks, 'A fucking *war?* I got a gun and I'm pushing Tone now, but these motherfuckers are talking about sending *everybody* into my house.' "

He brought up, as an example, the day Wiz got stabbed. "That's what I did to Jose," Tone told me. "I had Knickerbocker Avenue closed. I put 200 people on their block and said, 'Sell drugs now, motherfucker.' "

What if one of Jose's drug-dealer friends had pulled out a gun?

"I got to do it," Tone said. "If I didn't, they would have had the impression that Jose stabbed a King and nothing happened, and they could do it again. I got to show these guys, 'Yo, he got stabbed but don't get misled, we could kill him if we want to, we just don't choose to.' "

And if some Kings—tough Kings in jail, say—still don't feel that's good enough, Tone has to counterattack. "If you feel so strongly," he tells them, "you do justice in there."

And I wondered: Is that what he told the guys who stabbed Jose?

Tone's personal life is a mess. He lives with a girl named Sapphire in a five-room duplex in a public-housing complex in Coney Island, but there's barely any furniture, the parquet floor is badly corroded, and the kitchen sink leaks so badly they sleep downstairs. Plus, the lease is in Sapphire's mother's name, and she hates him—she was a guard at Rikers while he was a prisoner.

One day I drove Tone to Coney Island Hospital, where his infant daughter was sick with bronchitis. Tone picked her up and took her straight to the dayroom. "He doesn't even kiss me," Sapphire said. "He takes the baby and goes."

Sapphire is just seventeen, and Tone isn't legally married to her, so Tone's mother had to come sign the baby out. She carried an elaborate leather-bound Bible and didn't seem to approve of her son. "I believe in Jesus," she said. "He's the only King."

Finally, I got a chance to talk to Wiz himself. We stood in the back bedroom of his sister's apartment, cold winter light coming in the window, mattress on the floor, the train rumbling by on the El twenty feet from the windowpane. He told me he was twenty-one and his birth name was Frank Del Valle, that he dropped out of school in ninth grade, sold some drugs, did some stickups, then a prison bid for robbery and arson. He joined the Latin Kings two years ago, "for the unity."

He even liked the discipline. "It definitely put a lot of fucking knuckles on my head," he said. "I used to get physicals and everything for the stupid shit I used to do."

Like?

"Dumb shit, doing stickups in the avenue right there."

Then Wiz showed me his scars—an eraser-size puncture near his liver and the huge red welt the doctors carved on his belly. As he told the story, the three Kings Tone sent to confront Jose became six or seven. "We probably would have just beat his ass, you know what I'm saying, for talking," Wiz said. "If you're going to get into our shit, you're going to feel it."

Wiz talked about what it felt like to see a piece of his intestine hanging out of a hole in his belly—"Man, you should have seen that shit. It looked like a piece of braid." He cursed Jose's name—the motherfucker lived just four blocks away, and sometimes they bumped into each other on the street. But Wiz had no plans to take revenge himself. "Fuck it, he ain't worth it. He ain't worth destroying this whole beautiful nation that we have."

Back in the living room, Wiz's nephews were watching the Power Rangers. It was a poor apartment—plywood floor exposed in the kitchen, a broken fixture in the ceiling, a couple of tired velour chairs. But there was a feeling of warmth, and the smell of rice and beans on the stove, and four-year-old Marky denouncing his three-year-old brother Eric: "He's a punk and a puss!"

"I'm going to suspend you for two weeks for cursing," Tone said.

Defiant, Marky threw his crown.

"You can't throw your crown—you're suspended."

Marky threw it again.

"I'm going to strip you," Tone said.

"I'm a King!" Marky said.

When we left a half-hour later, Marky yelled after us: "I'm still a King!"

On Tone's thirtieth birthday, the Almighty Latin King Queen Nation showed up at St. Mary's Church in Harlem to celebrate. They lined up tribe by tribe and waited patiently, entering single file. A nineteen-year-old King named Gil manned the door, hugging each arrival and whispering in his ear: "You have any weapons?"

One guy handed over a sap—a sock with a combination lock inside.

By four, the church was jammed, about 300 Kings sitting in the pews and another 100 or 150 standing. On the stage, four men in orange sweats stood with their hands crossed. Two others held up gleaming swords. As speaker after speaker gave tribute, Tone sat on a throne, smiling and dandling his baby daughter on his knee.

One of the speakers was a surprise guest—the leader of the Connecticut Kings. In a dramatic statement, he said the Kings up in

Hartford were at war with a gang called Los Solidos. Many had died, and those who survived were bitter in their hearts. But now he was learning "from the brothers in New York" that peace was the better path. "So I am telling Tone today that as a birthday present for him, I will begin to meet with the Solidos," he said.

"*Amor de rey!*"

Another surprise! The leader of Los Solidos got up and shook hands with his enemy!

Another day, I talked to Herman Cintron Jr., the leader of Los Solidos up in Connecticut. He told me the war between the Solidos and the Connecticut Kings started in '93 when a Solido and a King fought over a girl. Two dozen men and a little girl have been killed. In fact, he was shot at just over the weekend, driving in his car. "Tell you the truth, I'm scared all the time," he said. "Tell King Tone to call us, 'cause we really need some help."

And another day, I met Tone and King Era at the Brooklyn Municipal Building, where Era was finally going to testify in the killing of Bishop Jr. Dressed in a white baseball cap and Tommy T-shirt, gold crown around his neck, Era was visibly nervous—as Tone said, "It ain't every day you walk into the D.A.'s office willingly."

But there he was, trying to do things right.

Then I overheard a striking detail, adding yet another layer of complexity to this endlessly complicated world: One member of the Kings contingent had a gun that night, and even shot at Bishop's killer as he escaped. Which was one reason Era didn't want to testify. So much for "If we had a gun, he would have been dead."

After months of hanging out with Tone, I still wasn't sure about him. Sometimes he seemed to be the perfect leader, a street-smart evangelist smuggling God's love under his tattoos. Sometimes he seemed to have too much street in him to go straight. And sometimes I would listen to his stream of glittering rap and think: *This guy's just a hustler.*

One thing is sure: The authorities won't back off any time soon. They don't seem to want to consider the possibility that Tone might be the real thing. As their prosecution gathered steam, the U.S. Attorney's office spun a piece of its organized-crime team into a new division called the Violent Gangs Unit. Early in January, the NYPD announced that the police would make fighting "youth gangs" their top priority in 1997. A few days later, the Bronx D.A. indicted three men in the shooting of Captain Plavnick. They weren't Latin Kings, but Assistant D.A. Dawn Florio blamed the Kings anyway—they had been offered $5,000 to kill a police captain in retaliation for the death of Anthony Baez, she said, and they had "subcontracted" the hit to members of the Netas. While this certainly seemed plausible—I remembered Tone saying, "If you feel so strongly, *you* do justice"—the D.A.'s case appeared to be based entirely on one unnamed confidential informant, and no Kings were indicted.

A week later, outside the Bronx courthouse, the Netas had a quick press conference. With six TV cameras rolling, Green Eyes called the arrests "a smoke screen to take attention away from the Livoti case" and said the arrested men weren't even Neta members. Ron Kuby invoked the FBI's COINTELPRO attack on the Black Panthers and said the police were trying to "foment gang violence" by pitting the Netas and the Kings against each other. Afterward, Tone lingered on the sidewalk with a group of Kings, huddling in the icy wind. He seemed subdued. Word on the street was that the cops' confidential informant was saying Tone personally handed off the $5,000 contract to the Netas. He turned to Kuby. "You know what I'm scared of? That this is the first felony in the RICO case they're building against me," he said.

"You should be scared," Kuby answered.

Tone grinned and gathered his men around him. Then they marched off into the South Bronx, looking for a place to get warm.

THE WASP WOMAN STUNG

Maybe she was just too short at only five feet, but Susan Cabot was being groomed as a starlet by Universal Pictures, even did a film with Humphrey Bogart. But when the big parts didn't come, she drifted into a B-movie world, then into a B-movie afterlife that eerily resembled her most famous movie—a recipe for madness, and for a very B-movie death.

A few hours before Susan Cabot was bludgeoned to death by her son, her psychologist happened to call to reschedule an appointment. He was shocked to hear her so despairing, he later testified in court: "I heard a tone in her voice that I had never heard before, and I had seen her depressed." She told him she wanted to die.

Cabot had fallen into one of those classic, dismal Hollywood afterlives. Once a starlet under contract to Universal Pictures, she had acted with Humphrey Bogart and Charles Bronson. She is said to have dated Marlon Brando and Rock Hudson, and her romance with King Hussein was national news in the late 1950s. But by the 1980s, she was living in a cluttered Encino, California, hilltop home with a disabled son. Police photos of the house show a jumble of detritus so thick, it must have been hard to walk through, with bags of newspapers in the bedroom and a chair and hamper in the bathtub. A regular visitor often found rats floating in the swimming pool.

Cabot had turned into something right out of *Sunset Boulevard* or *What Ever Happened to Baby Jane?* In her late fifties, she still wore her dresses low-cut and her makeup thick. Although she was only five feet tall—something her friends always thought had kept her from having a major career—she more than made up for it in presence. She was always glamorous and made a habit of dramatizing even the smallest details of her life. When guests came over, "she would just, I guess, almost act differently, like an actress would," her son told the court at his trial. "Just to try to be as glamorous as she could. I guess to impress them."

The way her psychologist, Carl Faber, diagnosed it, Cabot was one of those people "so disassociated from their life experience, they can't hold on to reality." It was exhausting to be with her. "You have to hold on to reality for both of you. And it winds up feeling like somebody is pulling it out of your bones."

Life had played Cabot a particularly cruel joke. Her best performance was in Roger Corman's *The Wasp Woman*. She played the title role, an aging cosmetics queen named Janice Starling, who tries to regain her youth (the better to advertise her product) by injecting herself with wasp venom supplied by a mad scientist. As a result of this Faustian bargain, she turns into a huge, bloodsucking insect.

By a baroque coincidence, her son, Timothy, received injections, too. Instead of younger, he wanted to be taller—or rather, his mother wanted him to be taller. Timothy (who declined to be interviewed for this article) was born with a dysfunctional pituitary gland. His body did not produce the necessary growth hormones or male hormones. A history of seizures and hypoglycemia had left him slightly handicapped (at twenty-four, he was still childlike, with a layer of baby fat and a slightly dazed, eager-to-please expression). At five, he had been diagnosed as suffering from dwarfism and was given shots that consisted of extracts drawn from the pituitary glands of human cadavers.

No wonder Susan Cabot was troubled. The confusion between illusion and reality is an actor's occupational hazard. But most actors lose themselves in dreams. Cabot lost herself in nightmares.

The year is 1951. The film is *The Enforcer*. Humphrey Bogart shoves a picture of Susan Cabot under the nose of a killer. From earlier glimpses, we know the face: dramatic, with high cheekbones, exotic dark eyes, and eyebrows so black and arched, they seem almost kinky. "Maybe this is the face that will haunt you," Bogart hisses. "Maybe these are the eyes that'll drive you crazy."

Bogart is investigating the murder of Cabot's character, asking the same questions real policemen would ask thirty-five years later: Who was she? Where did she come from?

"She came from out of town," her roommate tells Bogart. Beyond that, no one knows anything about her.

In real life as well, Cabot seemed to like it that way. Richard Miller acted with her in a series of Roger Corman B movies. "Usually someone would say, 'I'm going with somebody, this is the person I'm married to,' " Miller recalled. "None of that ever transpired with Susan. I didn't know where she lived; I didn't know who she saw. She'd come to the set, and that was it."

Cabot had reasons for her reticence. She was born Harriet Shapiro in Boston on July 9, 1927. Shortly after Cabot's birth, her mother was institutionalized with mental problems and her father abandoned the family. After that, Cabot lived in as many as fourteen foster homes, where she was "emotionally and sexually abused," said Faber in court. As a result, Cabot suffered from a kind of posttraumatic stress syndrome, he said. "She had extreme irrational terror, as abused children and war veterans do, about those experiences and was in and out of psychotherapy her whole adult life."

After moving from Boston to New York City, Cabot got interested in acting. As a student at Washington Irving High School, she wrote scripts and hung lights for the school drama club. The year she turned eighteen, she married Martin Eden Sacker, whom actress Kathleen Hughes remembers as an artist who made "somewhat gloomy paintings." After graduation, Cabot moved to Maine and joined a small theater group. At some point in the 1940s, she began landing television roles.

Her break came when impresario Max Arnow cast her as a Samoan maiden in Columbia Pictures' *On the Isle of Samoa*. Shortly afterward, Universal signed her to a four-year contract, and she went on to play a Sioux maiden in *Tomahawk*, an Apache maiden in *The Battle at Apache Pass*, and a Persian maiden in *Son of Ali Baba*. At Universal, Cabot became best friends with Hughes, then a fellow contract starlet at the studio. "In those days, Universal had classes—acting classes, dancing classes, horseback classes—so we were together all day," Hughes says. The two ingenues were sent on publicity tours together, to Texas, Oklahoma, and even once to Argentina. Friends from that period describe Cabot as smart, vivacious, creative, and above all, fun. She sang beautifully and was the hit of parties, with arias from *Tosca* or a belting version of "Summertime." "There were 9,000 parties every night," says Miller. "It was a light, happy, frothy time." He remembers Cabot as a good chess player, very pretty, and very intense. "She was always kind of uptight," he says. "It took a lot to relax her, to get her to be a calm person."

But Cabot would always be frustrated. At Universal, she never rose above the Indian-maiden roles, and when her contract expired, she went back to New York and appeared in a Broadway play, *A Stone for Danny Fisher*. She tended to speak in italics, using expressions like "totally mad." Even such good friends as Hughes found her "very, very vain, very self-centered, really preoccupied with her looks. She was incredibly talented, but she was incredibly neurotic."

Cabot was one of those women who invariably fall in love with the wrong man, Hughes says. "She seemed to go out of her way to have relationships with men that could come to no happy ending. She could never let anything go. [A romance] would be finished, and she would just go on and on about how she would never get over it. It just got annoying. She would never listen."

When Corman rediscovered Cabot on a trip to New York in the mid-1950s, she had been studying Method acting at the Neighborhood Playhouse. He brought her back to Hollywood and gave her over-the-top, melodramatic roles that suited her extravagant personality: an evil high priestess in *The Saga of the Viking Women and Their Voyage to the Waters of the Great Sea*, a disturbed coed in *Sorority Girl*, a moll in *Machine Gun Kelly*. "I really felt that she was one of those people who should have had a major career, and for whatever reason, a career did not take place," Corman says.

Cabot was more frustrated than ever. "She had a tremendous amount of talent, which wasn't being tapped," says Noel de Souza, an actor friend who used to join her for coffee. De Souza remembered her as volatile and troubled. Years later, Cabot told the horror-movie fanzine *Fangoria* that she had problems playing villains: "I loved it from the standpoint of their being a challenge, but it was very hard for me to play an unfeeling character—to do or say something cruel to another person, not feeling it in my bones or in my heart and know that the other person is suffering. I've been victimized by people like that, and it hurts."

Cabot often talked about being victimized. "She was very thoughtful about abuse," said Faber in court, "because she was an abused person, and the film business is often abusive." That was partly why she isolated herself in her house on the hill: "She couldn't take any more of that side of the ugliness of the world."

In 1959, Cabot finally quit the movie business for good. *The Los Angeles Times* ran a story in April of that year that said, "Pretty Susan Cabot abruptly flew to New York last night, ostensibly to audition for a part in a Broadway show." But friends said "the visit was prompted by her mushrooming romance with King Hussein, and most of her time in the East will be taken up by the youthful monarch." In her *Fangoria* interview years later, Cabot said she felt she had reached a dead end. "How many Wasp Women can you do?"

Shortly after she went to New York, Cabot dropped out of sight. One friend now says Hussein left her when he found out she was Jewish; that may have sent her into a tailspin.

The next four years of her life remain a mystery. The only hard fact is that she gave birth to Timothy Cabot in Washington, D.C., on January 27, 1964. It was a problem birth; Cabot had to have an emergency cesarean in the middle of surgery for a twisted intestine, and Timothy was born prematurely, weighing six pounds, four ounces, and suffering from jaundice. He was hospitalized for two and a half months. Cabot told friends that her son was the child of an English aristocrat or, alternately, the issue of an affair with a CIA or FBI agent who had gone on a mission and never returned. Later, a family attorney claimed that Timothy's father was King Hussein.

In any event, the abused child now had a child of her own, and she was proud. One of Timothy's doctors noted in a report that the boy spoke his first words and stood at twelve months: "The child does exceptionally well, especially with his artistic endeavors, according to his mother. He has an advanced vocabulary."

Just after he turned one, Timothy suddenly refused to eat. Fifteen hours later, he went rigid. For twenty minutes, he stared into space. Then he seemed to recover. There was another seizure a year later and more in the years to come. Cabot was convinced that Timothy was a "poor feeder." She became obsessed with his eating habits. She began mixing two eggs into his milk every day. She was afraid he wouldn't grow. Eventually, doctors decided the seizures were caused by acute hypoglycemia.

By this time, Cabot had returned to Los Angeles. Hughes believes Cabot was drinking heavily then and may even have been contemplating suicide. She apparently put that behind her when she married a businessman and former actor named Michael Roman, and Roman became Timothy's legal stepfather. Cabot (now Susan Cabot Roman) seemed to rally and began taking Timothy to schools and clinics. Most of them blamed Timothy's difficulties on a mixture of physical and emotional problems. A psychologist at UCLA observed, "Much of this youngster's immature behavior has been inappropriately reinforced by his mother. Mrs. Roman, being an actress, tends to be somewhat overly dramatic and overly concerned (i.e., 'Timothy couldn't walk down those huge stairs because of his short little legs')." By 1970, a mother's nightmare had become reality. Doctors at UCLA diagnosed Timothy's dwarfism.

In 1970, a UCLA doctor named Solomon Kaplan wrote to the National Pituitary Agency, asking permission to include Timothy in the test of a new growth hormone—the one extracted from corpses—arguing that the boy was an "unusual case." Timothy remained in the program for fifteen years.

One of Timothy's attorneys later referred to him as a "human experiment." But it was an experiment that apparently worked. Timothy made his mark on medical history by growing to the height of five foot four—four inches taller than his mother. At the trial, Timothy's doctor told the court that he was not a textbook case but "*the* classic textbook case. ... We used him to write the book." In fact, one textbook on diseases of the glands features a picture of Timothy, nude.

Nevertheless, Timothy would also have to take a combination of steroids, hydrocortisone, and testosterone. Actress Edith Fellows remembered visiting Cabot's Beverly Hills home in 1970. "The kitchen looked like a doctor's office," she says. Cabot talked of going back to acting, but "she didn't know if she could trust anybody to take care of the boy as well as she did."

In 1981, Cabot was divorced. A Los Angeles real estate broker named James Weinstock started tutoring Timothy that year and often spent the night in a spare room in Cabot's house.

In those years, Weinstock says, she was going to a therapist three or four times a week. The clutter had begun to accumulate—"Her house was stacked up with boxes, like some weird old lady's," he says. The house smelled of dogs—Cabot always had about ten dogs of exotic breeds, Shih Tzus or Akitas. She was well-off; Weinstock says she owned a Rolls-Royce, a Bentley, and a custom Mercedes-Benz. Though the source of her income is unclear, she often talked about being a self-made woman. "She was streetwise," Weinstock says. "She'd say, 'I'm a tough cookie, I did it by myself.' "

During that period, Cabot talked often of returning to show business, but she didn't like the idea of playing "mother parts," Weinstock says. "That's not how she conducted herself socially. She acted like a romantic lead." Weinstock says Cabot "liked young guys" and flirted suggestively at parties.

Timothy was getting deeper and deeper into martial arts. At times, he "would go into something akin to a catatonic state," Weinstock says, "where he would stand outside the door of his bedroom and swing those ninja sticks." His mother was overprotective, Weinstock thought. She wouldn't let him drive, for example, though he had a license. "He would want to do something with his friends, and she'd say, 'No, Timmy, you're different from other people.' "

For the next six years, Timothy and his mother lived alone in their house on the hill, among her junk and his kung-fu fantasies.

Hughes says Cabot's paranoia flared up at parties. She would angrily demand to know what people were saying, as if she feared they were talking about her. At one party, Hughes heard someone singing "Summertime," Cabot's old song, then was embarrassed to see Cabot come to the piano and take over, drowning out the other singer with her big voice. Hughes says, "It was a show-offy, nervy thing to do. She ruined somebody else's beautiful performance."

In 1983, a psychologist named Michael Carter became Timothy's tutor. By that time, the house was "very disheveled, very dirty, very unkempt," Carter said in court. He found Cabot "very up-and-down and very, very dramatic." Timothy would react by becoming "very muted, very passive." Although Timothy told the court she sometimes struck him, Carter insisted, "Tim never raised his voice to his mother."

There were other serious problems. Cabot had to regulate her son's many medications carefully. If his thyroid level dropped too low, he would fall into a lethargic state. If it rose too high, it would make him confused or agitated. Emotional stress also affected the mix—without a properly functioning pituitary gland, Timothy's body was unable to perform the routine chemical adjustments that ease stress in normal people.

Timothy's UCLA specialist was unhappy with Cabot's nursing abilities. "We believed she was not giving him his medication at times or not doing it according to the way we prescribed it," she said in court. Specifically, the boy kept coming in to the hospital with "very, very low" levels of male hormones. This kept his sexual functions and body hair to a minimum. Timothy's specialist thought Cabot was doing this on purpose, even going so far as to note her suspicions in Timothy's permanent medical record. One month before the killing, a blood test revealed a thyroid level so high, Timothy's doctor called Cabot in alarm and told her to reduce his dosage immediately.

Timothy's doctor said he had suffered some brain damage as a result of his glandular problems and his seizures as an infant. But his first lawyer argued—before he was replaced—that his mother's obsession with his height may have been partly to blame. In 1985, at least four people died from a tainted batch of hormones supplied by the Pituitary Agency. In court papers, the lawyer said that Timothy "reports that even after his mother received the 1985 warning, she had given him at least one and possibly more injections of the natural growth hormones on hand at the residence because of her interest in stimulating his growth."

In the weeks before Cabot's death, she had become even more erratic than usual, to the point where Timothy was "very frightened," his therapist testified. She had been talking about reviving her acting career, and Timothy said one day she decided she had to get into shape for the cameras. She borrowed a bar from one of Timothy's weight-lifting sets to get started. She also decided to sell her house. In her last two days, Timothy said, she suffered from asthma attacks that left her bedridden. Her psychologist testified that she was terrified that she and Timothy would end up penniless—a lifelong fear, he said, even though her estate eventually totaled about $1 million.

Cabot's old habit of asking the same question over and over had turned into a demand for "repetitive reassurance" so oppressive that she was often a—as Faber hesitantly characterized it in court—"provocative of anger." Put bluntly, she drove people crazy. "You would give a reassurance or you would explore it in a problem-solving way," he said, "maybe even suggest that one of the options might have more value than another. And the minute that you would be done with it, it was gone, and she would ask you all over; again, as if you hadn't said it. If I got exhausted in fifty minutes, Tim spent years in that house with her. I know that Susan must have brought those fears to Tim. They were together with that fear."

Cabot's depression and anxiety got worse and worse as the end approached. At about five o'clock on the last afternoon of Cabot's life, a real estate agent called about the house; she said Timothy told her his mother was too sick to come to the phone. Later that night, Cabot had begun to have some sort of nervous breakdown, Timothy told the court. "She was screaming," he said. "She was calling for her mother. She was just talking to herself."

Sometime that evening, Timothy finally tried to call the paramedics. His mother, he said, was infuriated: "Put the phone down, leave me alone," she screamed. According to her son, she was screaming so hard, she literally fell off the bed. As she regained her balance, he said, she reached for the heavy weight-lifting bar Timothy had lent her. "She picked it up and started swinging it at me," he told the court.

At this point, Timothy's memory started to get fuzzy. He couldn't remember if she'd actually hit him. "She might have grazed me or something," he said. "I tried to get it away from her. I think I grabbed it. And she still kept going."

Cabot grabbed a scalpel off her nightstand and attacked him with it, Timothy said. He paused in his tearful narration to explain that his mother carried the scalpel when she went for walks, using it to cut flowers she liked.

Finally the attorney asked the big question. "Do you recall hitting your mother with the bar?"

"The last thing I remember is trying to push her away from it," Timothy said. "Just to get out of that—to get out of that room."

Timothy called the police at 11:30 p.m. They arrived to find his mother face down on her bed, wearing a purple nightgown—a detail the newspapers picked up to paint a lurid picture of a fading glamour queen drowned in her Hollywood dreamworld. As if to keep the story tabloid, Timothy told the police detectives that a masked ninja warrior had broken into the house and knocked him out. But a few hours later, the police found the murder weapon in his room, buried in an oversize detergent box, and he soon confessed.

In court, Timothy's attorney asked him why he lied to the police. "Because I was scared," Timothy said. "I didn't want to be responsible. I didn't think anyone would understand the situation of what had happened."

In fact, just about everybody understood. Along with Faber, Cabot's mother, ex-mother-in-law, ex-husband, and friends all rallied to Timothy's side. So did the judge, reducing the original homicide charges to involuntary manslaughter and observing that "there was no question that the defendant loved his mother very much"—which earned the judge a mocking notice in *Newsweek*. Timothy's stepfather moved from New Orleans to Los Angeles to help his son recover. "It was a very, very trying life living with Susan," he says. "Extremely trying. And that's on the best of days." Hughes, Cabot's friend of thirty-six years, appeared to speak for everyone when she said, "This is such an awful thing to say, but after it came out that Timothy had done it, knowing Susan as well as I did, I thought if he did it, she must have had it coming."

Early one November morning three years after the 1986 killing, Timothy sat in court, literally on the edge of his chair, his face pale and tense. He had been released on bail after spending nearly three years in jail awaiting trial and seemed terrified at the prospect of going back. His aunt, grandmother, and a friend sat beside him. "You're making yourself sick," said his aunt. "You'e not going to go back." The friend squeezed his hand, saying, "There's every chance in the world you will not go back." Timothy's attorney strolled over to reassure him. "It'll be over today," he said.

But Timothy remained sitting stiffly on the edge of his chair. He stayed in the same position for the next half hour, until the judge sentenced him to three years' probation and time served, calling his mother's death "a tragic occurrence brought on by the bizarre and irrational behavior of the victim." There was a small notice in the newspaper.

Today Timothy is in better health. According to his stepfather, he has cut back on medications and his hypoglycemia is no longer a problem. Despite his unwillingness to be interviewed, he did say, "I'm trying to get away from the past and start a new life." He still dreams of doing special effects for the movies and is going back to school. And his mother exists only on the late show.

PERMISSIONS

"The Wasp Woman Stung" by John H. Richardson was first published in Premier in April 1991. Used by permission of the author.

"The Grifters, Part 1" by John H. Richardson was first published in Premier in December 1994. Used by permission of the author.

"The Grifters, Part 2" by John H. Richardson was first published in Premier in January 1995. Used by permission of the author.

"The Latin Kings" by John H. Richardson was first published in New York in February, 1997. Used by permission of the author.

"Not Guilty by Reason of Afghanistan" by John H. Richardson was first published in Esquire in February 2003. Used by permission of the author.

"Death of a Small-Timer" by John H. Richardson was first published in Issue 46 of the Columbia Journal in 2010. Used by permission of the author.

"El Gringo Loco" by John H. Richardson was first published in Playboy in May 2013. Used by permission of the author.

"The Gun King" by John H. Richardson was first published by the Marshall Project and Amazon Singles on August 28, 2018. Used by permission of the author.

ABOUT THE AUTHOR

John H. Richardson was born in Washington, D.C., in 1954. He grew up in Athens, Manila, Saigon, Washington, Seoul, Honolulu, and Los Angeles. He is a graduate of the University of Southern California '77 and Columbia University '82. His writing has appeared in the *Albuquerque Tribune*, *The Los Angeles Daily News*, *Premiere*, *New York*, and *Esquire*. He has taught at Columbia University, the University of New Mexico, and Purchase College and is the author of three books.

ABOUT THE PUBLISHERS

NeoText is a publisher of quality fiction and long-form journalism. Visit the NeoText website at NeoTextCorp.com

The Sager Group was founded in 1984. In 2012 it was chartered as a multimedia content brand, with the intent of empowering those who create art—an umbrella beneath which makers can pursue, and profit from, their craft directly, without gatekeepers. TSG publishes books; ministers to artists and provides modest grants; and produces documentary, feature, and commercial films. By harnessing the means of production, The Sager Group helps artists help themselves. For more information, please see TheSagerGroup.net.

ABOUT THE STACKS READER SERIES

The Stacks Reader Series highlights classic literary non-fiction and short fiction by great journalists that would otherwise be lost to history—a living archive of memorable storytelling by notable authors. Curated by Alex Belth and brought to you by The Sager Group.

MORE FROM THE SAGER GROUP

The Stacks Reader Series

The Cheerleaders: A True Story by E. Jean Carroll

An American Family: A True Story by Daniel Voll

Flesh and Blood: A True Story by Peter Richmond

An Accidental Martyr: A True Story by Chip Brown

Death of a Playmate: A True Story by Teresa Carpenter

General Interest

The Stories We Tell:
Classic True Tales by America's Greatest Women Journalists

New Stories We Tell:
True Tales by America's New Generation of Great Women Journalists

Newswomen: Twenty-five Years of Front Page Journalism

The Devil & John Holmes:
And Other True Stories of Drugs, Porn and Murder by Mike Sager

The Orphan's Daughter, A Novel by Jan Cherubin

Miss Havilland, A Novel by Gay Daly

Lifeboat No. 8: Surviving the Titanic by Elizabeth Kaye

Hunting Marlon Brando: A True Story by Mike Sager

The Swamp: Deceit and Corruption in the CIA
An Elizabeth Petrov Thriller (Book 1) by Jeff Grant

Meeting Mozart: A Novel
Drawn From the Secret Diaries of Lorenzo Da Ponte by Howard Jay Smith

More Books From The Sager Group

NeoText

THE SAGER GROUP
Artifex Te Adiuva

www.ingramcontent.com/pod-product-compliance
Lightning Source LLC
Chambersburg PA
CBHW030957210726
48290CB00007B/2344

9781958861004